LANGUAGE AND RELIGION

A semantic preface to a philosophy of religion

By the same author

Religious Faith, Language, and Knowledge
Faith and Moral Authority
The Symbols of Religious Faith
Moral Principles in the Bible

LANGUAGE
AND
RELIGION

A semantic preface to a philosophy of religion

by
BEN F. KIMPEL

PHILOSOPHICAL LIBRARY
New York

To my friend
JOHN NIGRO
Musician, scientist, inventor

CONTENTS

CONTENTS

Preface

This book is a study of some of the basic problems which arise in using language both for affirming religious faith and also for interpreting affirmations of religious faith. As such, it is a semantic analysis of the linguistic vehicle by means of which religious interpretations of reality are affirmed and reflected upon.

The reality which is interpreted by religious individuals constitutes the scope of religious faith, whereas the language used by religious individuals for affirming their interpretations constitutes the scope of a semantic analysis of religious faith. Such an analysis is often called "semiotical analysis," and according to this terminology, an analysis of language used in religious life may be classified as a semiotical study of religion.

According to a widespread contemporary point of view, philosophy itself is semiotical analysis, and the problems of philosophy are said to concern only "the semiotical structure of language." A semiotical analysis presupposes a knowledge of rules for constructing language expressions, and such rules constitute a grammar or syntax. It also presupposes a knowledge of rules for ordering sentences into a coherent system, and such rules constitute a logic. It in turn exemplifies rules for analyzing the meaning of such expressions, and these rules are neither the grammatical rules nor the logical rules according to which analyzed statements are individually formed and collectively ordered. They constitute rather a unique philosophical method for analyzing meaning affirmed in language. As a method for philosophizing, this method is also called "philosophical analysis," and according to many contemporary philosophers, it is the most significant development in modern philosophy.

As studies of language, semantics, or semiotics, or philosophical analysis, should not include any appraisal of the truth of interpretations affirmed by means of language. The only appraisal coming within their scope is the effectiveness of language for affirming interpretations, and such an appraisal is an evaluation of the adequacy of language for communicating interpretations. When, therefore, language analysts presume to appraise the truth of statements in theologies, or in creeds of religious faith, they do not confine themselves to the scope which they themselves specify as their special province. Passing judgment upon the knowledge-significance of religious interpretations does not come within the province of an analytic philosophy when it is delimited to an operation upon language for the purpose of understanding affirmed meaning. Passing such judgment comes within the scope rather of a theory of knowledge.

Although a particular philosophical analysis may presuppose a theory of knowledge, it must, nevertheless, be recognized that such a presupposition does not come within its scope as an analysis of language. A theory of knowledge is an interpretation of the extent of knowledge, and only when it is believed that language alone is knowable is it also logically maintained that possible knowledge is coextensive with an analysis of language. Presuming this, however, is not as such an analysis of language. It is rather presupposing something about the nature of reality which can be known, and this is maintaining a theory of knowledge. So likewise when it is maintained—as is frequently done in contemporary philosophies—that religious faith is not a way for knowing anything about the nature of reality, but is only an emotive expression of human life, a philosophy of religion itself determines what is thought about the significance of language affirmations of religious life.

4

Understanding language, however, includes taking account of its presumed function; and in the case of religious life, this is stating interpretations of ultimate reality. When one understands such interpretations as they are affirmed in language, he understands what religious individuals believe as the creed of their religious faith. And in so far as one understands such affirmations of religious faith, his understanding of them may contribute to his own religious faith. As a procedure for understanding affirmations of religious faith, a semantical analysis of this type is, therefore, practical. But as a philosophy stating a procedure for such understanding, it is theoretical.

In so far as religious faith is enlightened of the nature of reality, the language which articulates religious faith is a means for acquiring knowledge of reality. In understanding what enlightened religious life affirms about ultimate reality, one may thus become enlightened about ultimate reality. Understanding such affirmations is then significant for two reasons—both for understanding the meaning of affirmations of religious faith, and also for knowing something about reality, interpretations of which constitute the meaning of affirmations of enlightened religious faith.

The point of view maintained in this book is that an enlightened religious interpretation has the same knowledge-significance whether or not it is *affirmed* in language. Language is not essential for having enlightened beliefs—and so for having knowledge—although it is essential for *affirming* them. Language is a vehicle for articulating interpretations, but interpretations communicated by language are not only about language. If they were, there would be no empirical knowledge. There would be only knowledge about language expressions, and so only analytical knowledge. An *affirmed* interpretation is a language expression, whereas an interpretation which is informed of realities other than language is an intelligible type of experience even though it is not affirmed.

5

Language used for affirming religious beliefs is the only data which is relevant for a semantical study of religion. Yet, since religious individuals affirm interpretations of realities other than language, a semantical analysis of religion must take account of this fact. And recognizing that there is such an intended reference to ultimate reality is taking account of the "factual reference" in religious life. Or more accurately stated, it is taking account of the ultimate reality, of whose nature they presume knowledge.

The objective of a philosophy of religion which employs the method of semantical analysis is clarifying the meanings of assertions made by religious individuals, just as the objective of a philosophy of science which uses the same type of semantical procedure is clarifying the meanings of assertions made by scientists. A semantical analysis of language is a clarification of the meanings of language expressions, and as such, contributes to an understanding of affirmed meaning rather than to an increase of meaning, or to an extension of the field of significant interpretations. Extending the range of significant interpretations of physical reality, for instance, is the specific contribution of the physical sciences to human life, whereas extending the range of significant insights into the nature of ultimate reality is the specific contribution of religious faith to human life.

The substance of this book was given in public lectures for the Graduate School of Drew University. I should, therefore, like to acknowledge my indebtedness to Dr. Stanley R. Hopper, Dean of the Graduate School, for inviting me to deliver these lectures.

I am especially indebted and very grateful to my colleague in philosophy, Mr. Robert Boyll, who has helped me immeasurably in thinking through this study; in correcting the manuscript; and in reading the proofs.

B. K.

The Graduate School, Drew University.

6

Chapter I

A PHILOSOPHY OF LANGUAGE IN RELIGION

1. *A philosophy about language in religion presupposes a philosophy of religion*

A widespread point of view in modern philosophies of lauguage is that the *sole* function of language in religion is expressive of feelings. Such a point of view, for example, is affirmed by Ogden and Richards, who declare that "it ought to be impossible to talk about . . . religion as . . . capable of giving 'knowledge'" since all language in religious life expresses only feelings.[1]

This point of view, however, is not only a philosophy about language, but also a philosophy about religion. A philosophy of religion, in fact, is presupposed in maintaining that the exclusive function of language in religion is expressive. Such a philosophy of religion, in turn, presupposes a philosophy of knowledge that whatever is affirmed as religiously significant is an expression only of feelings.

In maintaining that the only function of language in religion is expressive, one believes that the sole objective of religious life is achieved in having feelings. This interpretation of the role of language is, therefore, a particular version of the more general premise that religious life achieves its objective within experience itself. Malinowski, for example, maintains that all religiously significant activities fulfil no purpose beyond their expression; and he cites the "celebration of a birth" as such an activity, having "no purpose," but expressing "the

7

feelings of the mother, the father, the relatives." The position, however, that "in the religious ceremony there is no purpose directed toward a subsequent event" is not arrived at as a result of observing religious life.[2] It is rather a premise according to which aspects of human life are *classified* as religious. The affirmation that the function of "self-contained acts" is "achieved in their very performance" is a definition, since it specifies how the term "self-contained" is used.[3] Yet, in *selecting* elements of religious life as "self-contained" acts, this definition itself becomes the basis for a procedure in classifying acts as religious—since only those acts are selected as religious which are assumed to be purely expressive. And in assuming this, religious experience is prejudged by the assumption itself.

What impels a person to reflect about the soundness of this assumption, however, is the fact that reflective religious individuals deny its soundness. They maintain that they use language not only for expressing their feelings, but also for articulating their interpretations about the nature of ultimate reality which they revere and worship. When, therefore, an interpreter of religion dismisses all religious affirmations as *merely* expressive, he prejudges the reflective competency of religious individuals by implying that they are incapable of distinguishing feelings from interpretations which they presume to be true. Moreover, when one maintains that the *sole* function of language in religion is expressive of feelings, he actually regards all religious interpretations of reality as misinterpretations. Although this procedure in disparaging religious claims to knowledge is often looked upon as "empirical," the only aspect of it which is "empirical" is the experience it interprets. Prejudging such experiences, however, has nothing whatever in common with an empirical procedure. A procedure is accurately classified as "empirical" only when it is a method for understanding interpreted data. And religious faith is not *empirically* interpreted when it is dogmatically

8

maintained that its affirmations about ultimate reality are *in principle* unsound.

If no intelligent person were religious, there would indeed be some empirical basis for assuming that religious faith is possible only when intelligence is at a minimum. But it is a fact that some philosophically trained individuals respect religious faith as one of the means, or one of the ways, by which human life is enlightened about reality. This fact, therefore, cannot be dismissed as having no philosophical significance, since it is impressive that a reflective person can both understand the affirmations of religious faith, and can also esteem them as warranted in light of all that he knows.

Although there may well be experiences which are superficially similar to religious faith, no one has religious faith unless he is convinced that his interpretations of ultimate reality are true; and his reverence for a reality esteemed as ultimate is itself one expression of his conviction that his ideas about its nature are true. Reverence for such a reality is a religious attitude or feeling, and so cannot be thought of as true, since the term "true" has no meaning in reference to attitudes or feelings, but only in reference to propositions. A religious person, however, believes his interpretations of reality are true propositions, and his conviction that they are is his confidence in the truth of beliefs which constitute the idea-content of his faith.

Faith is affirmed as warranted when it is believed that a religious interpretation of life and the world is sound. The belief, however, that it is sound is not a certification of its warrant, since such certification is not within the province of human life. And, therefore, it is not within the scope either of religious faith or of philosophical reflection. A religious person is confident that his faith is sound; and yet, in so far as he is capable of reflecting, he thinks about its soundness. Affirmations of religious faith are primarily about the nature of a reality esteemed as ultimate, and although a religious

9

person respects his affirmations about such a reality as true, there is no way for him to subject his faith to what is often called an "impartial" or "objective" evaluation. A reflective individual can, however, compare the *affirmations* of his faith with all the evidence of which he is able to take account; and when he does so, he takes advantage of all that comes within the range of his philosophy. Reflecting upon the *affirmations* of religious faith is not converting religious faith into philosophy. It is rather adding to religious faith the reflections of a religious life. In so far as anyone understands his religious faith, he is aware that he is not religious simply because he is reflective or philosophical. He is aware rather that he is religious and also philosophical. His religious faith is not a product of his reflecting; yet, in reflecting on his faith, he clarifies his faith. And his respect for his faith deepens as he becomes convinced of its soundness in light of the evidence upon which he reflects.

Philosophy is reflecting; and one who philosophizes may reflect upon the affirmations of religious faith which are one part of what Plato calls "the stream of speech . . . which ministers to intelligence." [4] And in devoting himself to a sympathetic understanding of another's affirmations of religious faith, he may indirectly understand what another may more directly believe, or even know; and this increase in enlightenment is made possible only by means of language. Although reflecting upon *affirmations* of religious faith is not itself religious faith, it is at least a step which may be included in the earnest efforts of an individual to become enlightened. One becomes enlightened to the extent that he understands what an enlightened person affirms, and in so doing, he becomes enlightened not only about what another says, but also about the reality which the other interprets.

The more one knows about the nature of the world and life, the more is he able to understand the basic affirmation of religious faith that the world and life are related to an ulti-

10

mate reality upon which both are finally dependent. A comprehension of the significance of such an ultimate reality for human life is, therefore, as much an aspect of an individual's philosophy as it is of his religion. This is not saying that a person's religion is of the same significance to him as his philosophy. It is only saying that in growing in the profundity of religious life by comprehending the nature of life and the world in relation to a reality revered as ultimate, an individual grows in the depth of his philosophy. And in so far as a religious person endeavors to understand the reality he worships, he clarifies his ideas about it. In so doing, his philosophy contributes to his religious life.

Philosophical reflections about religion may well be one element in a reflective person's life, although a philosophy of religion is not a religion. It is only a reflection about religion. Although philosophy and religion are distinct from each other, they nevertheless are closely related in all who seek to understand the nature of the world in which they live. If this is the case, then the reflections of a philosophical person on the nature of ultimate reality are understandable to every religious person who also strives to know something of the nature of ultimate reality. This again is not saying that philosophy is religion. It is only saying that no intellectually serious person desires to worship with less understanding than he can possibly achieve; and such a person regards achieving knowledge of ultimate reality by every means within his grasp as a condition for his worship. Every means which man may employ for understanding something about the cosmic setting in which he lives is a contribution to his reverence for the reality whose glory the heavens declare, and whose handiwork the world reveals.

When scientific methods are used for gaining knowledge of the world in order that one may be aware of its nature as an expression of a reality other than the world, then the methods of science are also enlisted in the service of religious life. But the methods of science require this significance only by virtue of the way their role is interpreted, since there is no religious way of employing scientific methods. Methods referred to as the procedures of the sciences are techniques by means of which a non-religious person may acquire as much information of an aspect of reality as a religious person may acquire who uses the same techniques with equal skill. Yet, the *significance* of such knowledge for both individuals may differ in so far as each interprets his knowledge from a different perspective. A religious person may interpret his knowledge of the world which he gains by the procedures of science as enlightening him of more than the world; and when he does, his use of science is not merely an incidental addition to his knowledge. It is rather the basic premise in terms of which he interprets the significance of his knowledge.

In so far as affirmations of religious faith are about a reality, or an aspect of reality, which is not interpreted in the range of science, the *affirmations* of religious faith are not equivalent to *statements* in science. Although not equivalent, in the sense that one cannot be substituted for the other, both may, nevertheless, be included in an interpretation which is more comprehensive than either without the other. The basic premise of religious faith is independent of science, and procedures in science are independent of religious interpretations. But when an individual having religious faith is aware of the contribution of the procedures of the sciences to a knowledge of the world in relation to the reality he worships as ultimate, he uses them from a perspective which he does not acquire from scientific procedures.

An affirmation, for example, about the sun as a condition for life on the earth is regarded as a factual statement in physical science, whereas an evaluation of the significance of life on the earth, made possible by a function of the sun, is not even within the province of physical science. Yet, it is within the province of man's interpretation. And so every

12

individual who ventures an interpretation about its significance does so not as a scientist, but as an interpreter of the knowledge gained by means of science.

The more an individual knows of the nature of the physical world, the richer is the meaning of the *term* "physical world" for him. The meaning of this term for a religious individual, however, is not an achievement of his faith, but of his science. What an individual knows of the physical world may in turn be interpreted in the perspective of his religious faith, which is cognitively significant to him because presupposing a body of ideas with which the significance of the physical world is interpreted. Religious faith, therefore, is not affirmed as a supplement to scientific and philosophical interpretations. When the ultimate reality is revered as God, man's reverence for God is thus integral to his reflections upon life and the world.

2. *A philosophy about language in religion must be distinguished from affirmations of religious faith*

Philosophies about religious faith often use critical terms as they are not used in religious life, since the basic premise of some philosophies is not the premise of religious faith. Hobbes, for example, acknowledges that men speak about God as "eternal" and "infinite," but he maintains that by these terms men do not "declare what God is" since "that were to circumscribe Him within the limits of our fancy."[5] It must be pointed out, however, that the terms which men use for affirming interpretations of God do not circumscribe God. They circumscribe only human life when they are less enlightened of God's nature than it is possible for them to be. When, for example, it is said that "God's existence is based entirely on our belief," the reality spoken about is not the object of religious faith. The *sense* of the term "God" is indeed "based entirely on our belief"; but the *existence* of God is in no way dependent upon "our belief."

Some philosophers, however, are more impressed with man's beliefs than with realities whose nature may inform some of his beliefs. A religious person, on the other hand, regards his idea of God as an interpretation of a reality other than human life. It is, therefore, not surprising that there is misunderstanding when a philosopher uses terms of a religious vocabulary with senses which they do not have in religious life. Jaspers, for example, declares: "The voice of God lies in the self-awareness that dawns in the individual, when he is open to everything that comes to him from his tradition and environment."[6] In declaring that philosophizing is learning how "to rise to godhead—or to know being qua being," Jaspers uses the term "godhead" for referring to a level of experience, but not to a reality other than experience by which the level of life is lifted in relation to it.[7]

According to Jaspers, man becomes aware of himself in philosophizing, and in so becoming aware of his own nature, he achieves a level of life which is spoken of in the terminology of religious life as "godhead." In raising the level of life to that "level of being capable of speaking with this God," "The godhead is drawn to us in its aspect of personality."[8] This all sounds as if it were an affirmation about the relation of human life to a reality other than human life. Yet, this would be misinterpreting Jaspers for he specifically says that this achievement is a "way of man's self-assertion through thinking." What he means, therefore, is clarified in being told that such *a type of life* is "authentic being," and that having "deep roots in authentic being" is "the judgment of God."[9]

A basic source of confusion in reading some philosophies of religion is asssuming that their terminology is used with the meanings given by religious faith. The phrase, for example, "to live by God," means, according to Jaspers, "to live as though we staked our existence on the assumption that God is." [10] One would indeed be helped in understanding what this means if he were, for instance, to know a philosophy such as Vaihinger's interpretation of Kant, according to which, religious life is acting "as if" or "as though" men "staked (their) existence on the belief that God is." Although this is a distorted version of religious faith, such an analysis of religious faith is, nevertheless, inevitable in a philosophy which assumes that no language is informative of a reality other than human life. And in maintaining that there can be no knowledge of a reality other than human life, it denies the presumed cognitive role of language in religious life, which presumed role, however, is a premise of religious faith itself. In denying its soundness, it thus dismisses religious faith as a means for contributing to man's knowledge of the total context in which he lives—which context includes not only human life and the physical world, but a reality more ultimate than both.

3. *Language in philosophies of religion is often ambiguous*

Religious faith as interpreted in this study is a way in which an individual relates himself to a reality he reveres as ultimate. So regarded, it is interpreted as a condition for achieving knowledge of a reality which is believed to be other than experience. The possibility, however, for achieving knowledge of such a reality is denied by those who maintain that knowledge is limited to experience.

When one believes that experiences alone are knowable, he speaks, for example, of the "strength to live by faith," and by this he does not mean securing strength from a reality other than experience. [11] He means rather that faith as experience is itself a source of strength. Thus a *term* such as "faith" which is used in interpreting religion can be understood only when one understands the philosophy itself which is presupposed in interpreting religion. A reflective person has a philosophy,

15

and in using a term about whose meaning he has reflected, he employs a philosophy. Jaspers, for example, declares: "Reflection on God clarifies our faith." By this he means that in reflecting on faith, one clarifies *faith*.[12] Marcel likewise does not regard faith as a way of relating human life to a reality other than human life when he declares: "Our point of reference can be based only upon experience itself, treated as a massive presence which is to be the basis of all our affirmation."[13] One hardly need point out that Jaspers and Marcel do not mean the same by "faith" as does a person who believes that in his faith he is related to a reality *other than experience*, of whose nature he is acquainted by means of experience.

A metaphysic, according to Marcel, is not an interpretation of a reality other than human life, since the reality about which an individual reflects in formulating his metaphysic is experience—of which there are many types. Pride is one. Hence, Marcel speaks of "the metaphysical problem of pride."[14] Faith is another. Hence, he affirms that "fidelity is ontological in its principle."[15] In thus speaking about the "eminent ontological value to be assigned to fidelity," he speaks about a type of experience.[16] In delimiting the scope of a metaphysic to experience, however, he declares that "we tend, without realizing it, to form far too restrictive an idea of experience"—and this may well be the case.[17] Yet, this possible failure in no way makes a difference in what Marcel regards as the scope of *possible knowledge,* which, according to him, is experience itself.

The metaphysic of religious faith—as religion is interpreted in this study—is not an analysis exclusively of experience. Religious faith as experience includes an interpretation of a reality which is revered as ultimate; and such an interpretation is itself a metaphysic. According to this interpretation of religion, therefore, the "fundamental fact" of religious faith is that there is an ultimate "Being" to which one is related. Using

16

a comparable terminology, however, Marcel affirms; "Being 'involved' is the fundamental fact." [18] According to him, the fundamental fact which concerns a reflective person is "being involved"; and "being involved" is a type of living, or a type of experience.

What is of utmost concern, however, for one who desires knowledge of a reality other than experience is whether faith is a means for enabling him to acquire such knowledge. But when an achievement of such knowledge is denied *in principle,* a philosophical premise is affirmed which contradicts the very premise which is basic to religious faith itself.

Religious faith is an experience, and in acknowledging this, one admits that a psychology of religion is one way for taking account of the significance of religious faith in human life. But such a psychology of religious faith is not equivalent to the affirmations which constitute religious faith. Psychology is a study of experience, and as such, it is not an interpretation of ultimate reality. Religious faith, on the other hand, is an interpretation of ultimate reality, and so includes a conviction about the truth of interpretations of such a reality. In so far, however, as one insists that religious faith can be understood in terms of experience alone, he maintains that a psychology of religion has the last word about the role of religious faith. Yet in believing that a psychology of religion is an adequate interpretation of the *role* of religious faith, one repudiates religious faith as a way for relating human life to a reality other than human life, and so it also repudiates the cognitive presumption of religious faith. This cognitive presumption, however, is itself a basic premise of religious faith.

4. *Language is commonly misused in affirming religious faith*

A language with which religious faith is affirmed may also be a source for misunderstanding religious faith. Even so fundamental a word in a vocabulary of religious life as "divine" is frequently misused, as for example, when St. Thomas declares: "Sacred doctrine derives its principles, not from any human knowledge, but from the divine knowledge." [19] Since any knowledge affirmed in doctrine is human, the term "divine" in this affirmation is misplaced. "Divine knowledge" is not the means by which "all our knowledge is ordered" because man is not in possession of "divine knowledge." Man may well know divine reality; but whatever he knows about its nature is not "divine knowledge." It is human knowledge about divine reality.

Man likewise is familiar with human language, and with no other. Yet, a modern writer in the philosophy of language and religion declares: "The religious symbol is always supernatural in all the possible meanings of this word." [20] The adjective "supernatural" in this statement is obviously misplaced. No symbol employed in religious life is supernatural. Only the referent of religious life is "supernatural." In so far as a religious person uses language either in affirming his faith, or in reflecting about the affirmations of his faith, he must, therefore, be careful to preserve the unique senses of terms which are critical in a vocabulary of religious faith itself. The basic vocabulary of religious faith consists of critical terms in religious life; and these must be used with utmost care. Included in this critical vocabulary are the terms "divine," "supernatural," "ultimate," "unconditioned," "transcendent," "infinite," and others whose specific role in religious life is referring to a reality esteemed as "first"; and, therefore, revered as no other reality is revered.

In so far as the term "supernatural," or "supranatural," designates "the Lord, the first," who made "heaven and earth," it refers to an order of existence which is time-independent. "Time-independent," in turn, is the minimum sense of the term "eternal" used for referring to reality worshipped in

18

religious faith. The point emphasized here, however, is not primarily a matter of the metaphysic of religious faith, but rather a matter of the vocabulary for affirming religious faith.

The minimum sense of the term "eternal" in a vocabulary for affirming religious faith is "independent of temporal sequence." Yet, this minimum sense is ignored when the term is used for speaking about realities which are never thought of as time-independent. Jaspers, for example, declares: "Plato teaches the *eternal* . . . experiences of philosophy." Since there is nothing about the sequence of human experiences which is eternal, Jaspers misuses the term. But in charging him with such misuse one believes that there is a reality other than human experience, of whose nature something is knowable. Yet, in so far as Jaspers follows Kant, he does not believe there is such a knowable reality, and so uses the term "eternal" in speaking about a quality of experiences.

In speaking about religious experience as "the state of being ultimately concerned," Tillich also uses a critical word in a vocabulary of religious life as an adjective for a reality which is not worshipped. If religion is interpreted in terms of "concern," it may be spoken of as concern for the ultimate, or concern expressed in reverently relating life to a reality esteemed as ultimate; but it should not be defined as "ultimate concern." In declaring that "the religious aspect (of human life) points to that which is ultimate, infinite, unconditional *in man's spiritual life,*" Tillich thus uses the term "unconditional" as he uses the term "ultimate"; and he uses neither of these terms as adjectives of a reality worshiped in religious life.[21] He uses them rather as adjectives of human life.

The term "transcendent" is commonly used as if its sense were clear; and yet, such an assumption is as indefensible in regard to this term, as it is in regard to most other terms in the vocabularies both of religion and of philosophies of religion. Jaspers, for example, speaks about man's "dependence on transcendence" as "the only independence possible for us," and declares that "Only transcendence can make this questionable life good." [22] The transcendence, of course, of which he speaks is a reference within human life, and in speaking about "a summons to transcendence," he refers to a *quality of life* which an individual may achieve in referring beyond what his life already is to what it may become. When the term "transcendence," therefore, is used for designating a type of human experience, it obviously has a very different sense from what it has in referring to the nature of God.

The term "infinite" in religious affirmations is likewise equivocal. When Kierkegaard declares that "certainty can be had only in the infinite," he apparently uses the term "infinite" for designating ultimate reality. But when he says that "Nothing historical can become infinitely certain for me except the fact of my own existence (which again cannot become infinitely certain for any other individual who has infinite certainty only of his own existence)," he uses the term both as an adverb characterizing man's acting, and also as an adjective characterizing man's activity. [23] The equivocal nature of this term as used by Kierkegaard is unmistakably obvious in declaring that "striving is infinite; that is, it is directed toward the infinite," since in this case, the term "infinite" qualifies both religious life and the reality to which religious life is directed. In declaring, however, that "infinite thought is so infinite," Kierkegaard does not even use the term equivocally, because this expresion is purely emotive or expressive. And it is just such a use of language which is cited by unsympathetic critics of religion as discrediting *in principle* the cognitive function of language in religious life.

The term "religion" is itself carelessly used, and when it is so used, it is not surprising that almost anything is said about religion, as for example, that "religion demands the existence of seasonal, periodical feasts." [24] But a moment's reflecting enables one to realize that in the name of religion,

20

men designate certain seasons for special ceremonies—which may well be the most appropriate ways they can conceive for relating themselves to the reality they revere as supremely worthy of their worship. Yet such ceremonies are men's activities; and religion as an aspect of human life includes them, but it does not "demand" them. The affirmation likewise that "religion standardizes the right way of thinking and acting" is equally inaccurate.[25] As an institution, religion is a standardizing of one aspect of human life, although it is not religion which does the standardizing. Religion as one aspect of human life includes all that men do in earnestly endeavoring to relate themselves to the reality which they esteem as ultimate. In the crises of life, therefore, it is not "religion (which) steps in"; but in such crises, religious men turn to a reality they trust for its supreme dependability. Religion is not trusted as the one reality which is dependable as all else is not, but it includes all that men do in relating themselves to the reality they revere as supremely trustworthy. Thus both religion and religious faith are misinterpreted when it is said, for example, that "man's conviction of continued life" is "one of the supreme gifts of religion."[26] Faith in a reality esteemed as supremely worthy of man's trust in life and in the hour of death is not a "gift of religion." Rather, religion as an aspect of human life includes the faith that man is related to such a reality which is not subject to death.

The term "religion," however, is often used to refer to an aspect of human life which is devoid of religious faith, such as magic, which includes all that men do in expressing their conviction that they themselves possess the means sufficient for attaining the goods which they supremely desire. When, for example, it is believed that by reciting a prayer ten times one can secure what he could not secure by devoutly praying once, he believes in the effectiveness of prayer as a language formula. Affirming scriptural passages any number of times a day is certainly not an equivalent for religious faith, although

21

it may well be faith in the efficacy of words. Confidence in the practical efficacy of a language itself with which a prayer is articulated is indeed one type of faith; whereas confidence that prayer is a means for relating life to the *ultimate* source of good is a very different type of faith.

A religious person having faith in God as the ultimate source of good likewise does not turn for renewal to "a store house of peace producing experiences." [27] The reality to which he turns in complete trust is other than human life, and other than human possessions. A so-called "peace" secured by a technique of manipulating language, therefore, is as remote from religious faith as any element in human life can be. Yet, developing a so-called "new mental slant" by means of repeating a passage from Scripture may well be as much of religious faith as many in a modern age of magic are capable of understanding.

In affirming that "it is well to study prayer from an efficiency point of view," one indeed gets a very clear understanding of a level of life, which in desperation resorts to techniques copied from religious life, even though such techniques are often used without religious faith. Although "enthusiasm for faith power" may well be "absolutely boundless" among members of some flourishing fads and contemporary cults, one must, nevertheless, wonder just what is meant by the ambiguous expression, "faith power," and he gets a very clear analysis of it in the affirmation that "the secret is to fill your mind with *thoughts* of faith." [28] What is thus recommended as a beneficial "technique" is *thoughts* of faith. Faith in an idea, however, is not religious faith; and so the recommended procedure, "First the idea, then faith in *it*," must be classified as an aspect of magic rather than religion.

Distinctions such as these would not be worth considering if they were merely incidental in a language which is used for speaking about religion. They express, however, basic types of thinking about religion; and in so far as they do, they are essential for stating a philosophy of religion. Although this study is only a preface to such a philosophy, it, or a comparable analysis, is, nevertheless, an indispensable preface, since affirmations of religious life, and so a philosophy about religious faith, are articulated in language. And neither can be understood apart from a critical study of language.

Chapter II

AMBIGUITIES IN PHILOSOPHIES
OF KNOWLEDGE

1. *Critical terms in philosophies of knowledge are often ambiguous*

The primary objective of a philosophy of religion is understanding affirmations of religious faith. Yet, much which often constitutes a philosophy of religion falls short of this modest goal; and one factor in accounting for this is the carelessness with which language is used in stating a philosophy of religion. A philosophy about the relations of faith and knowledge, for example, cannot be clear unless the sense of the term "knowledge" itself is clear. An awareness, however, that the sense of this critical term is not clear underlies the comment made by Ogden and Richards that the term is "no longer of much service in philosophies." Yet, it must be pointed out that unless the term "knowledge" is used with a clear meaning, there is no sound basis for affirming, *as they do,* that "it ought to be impossible to talk about . . . religion . . . as capable of giving 'knowledge.'" [1] Deleting this term from a philosophical vocabulary for interpreting religion is thus a sound procedure only when its sense has been clarified. And unless this term is used with a clear sense, there is no sound basis for rejecting it either from a vocabulary of religious life or from a philosophy about religion.

The term "knowledge," however, cannot be deleted from an interpretation of the nature of religion simply on the

24

grounds of semantic considerations alone. When its deletion is recommended, it is always on the grounds of a philosophy of religion as well as a philosophy of knowledge. Thus Ogden and Richards presume both a philosophy of religion and also a philosophy of knowledge when they maintain that the term "knowledge" ought not to be used in speaking about religion. A basic presupposition of their philosophy is that whatever is referred to as "knowledge" does not include an aspect of religious life. Hence their recommendation for restricting the term "knowledge" in speaking about religion does not rest upon the presumed ambiguity of this term, but rather upon its presumed unsuitability for referring to any aspect of religious life.

This presumption is not primarily a premise of a philosophy about the nature of language, but about the nature of religion. Repudiating the use of the term "knowledge" in referring to an achievement peculiar to religious life is a semantic procedure, although the basis for this procedure is a presumption about religion. Before the use of this term, however, can be restricted as a matter of principle in interpreting religious life, something must first be assumed about religious life. It must first be assumed that there is nothing in religious life which in any way parallels what is referred to as "knowledge" in other aspects of life—such as in the sciences, or in our daily experiences.

Yet, when one even speaks about having knowledge "in daily experiences," he uses two critical terms, neither of which is unambiguous. In classifying knowledge as experience, one takes for granted that the term "experience" is a means for clarifying the term "knowledge," but this is an unsound presumption. The aspect of life to which we refer when we use the term "experience" is no more clearly understood than is the aspect of experience to which we refer when we use the term "knowledge."

It may well be, as Bertrand Russell maintains, that "much

too much fuss is made about 'experience.'"[2] Yet, one cannot intelligently either agree or disagree with this assertion without having some understanding of the sense with which the term "experience" itself is used. In saying, for example, that one *"knows"* experience, he speaks about one type of experience in terms of another type of experience. The experiences we know constitute one type of experience, and knowing them is another type of experience. One hardly need continue this analysis, since it is obvious that critical terms in the vocabularies of some philosophies are no clearer than the same terms in vocabularies which do not presume to be "philosophical." This is not disparaging philosophy. It is merely acknowledging that philosophers are faced with a problem of language when they affirm their reflections.

In affirming that "all the materials of . . . knowledge" are "from experience," Locke, for example, merely stipulates a language procedure for delimiting the term "knowledge" to the range of the term "experience."[3] But such a procedure is not an analysis of the term "experience" by which the term "knowledge" is defined.

Affirmations are commonly made in philosophies about "objects of experience" as the basis for knowledge. Yet, a moment's reflection on these affirmations makes one aware of the ambiguity of the critical expression "objects of experience." This expression, in fact, is used with as many meanings as there are theories of knowledge. What Locke means by "objects of experience," for example, are realities other than experience. What Hume means by "objects of experience" are organized experiences. In analyzing organized experiences, Hume, therefore, maintains that nothing is known about anything other than features of experience.

Both Hume and Kant maintain that we know "objects of experience," but Kant, unlike Hume, believes that our experiences are organized by *a priori* capacities. In believing this, he is a rationalist; whereas Hume, in maintaining that these

26

capacities are acquired in having experiences, is a radical empiricist. By the expression, "objects of experience," Locke, on the other hand, means what neither Hume nor Kant means, since he believes that there are realities other than experiences, something of whose nature is knowable in experience. Thus, if one should know nothing of the history of philosophies other than the ways in which Locke, Hume, and Kant use the expression, "objects of experience," he would readily understand that an affirmation about "objects of experience" is so ambiguous it may with justification be called "semantically vacuous." Capable of meaning anything, it actually means nothing that is unambiguously clear. For this reason, the term "experience" has rightly been referred to by Professor Whitehead as "one of the most deceitful in philosophy." [4]

"Objects of sense" are often said to be "objects of knowledge." Yet, the expression, "objects of sense," is as ambiguous as the expression, "objects of experience." By the expression, "objects of the senses," Kant means organized sensory experiences, and this meaning is unambiguously affirmed when he maintains that "objects of the senses . . . exist only in experience." [5] Although Kant takes for granted that there are realities other than experiences, he, nevertheless, denies that anything of their nature is knowable. Thus in declaring that "We know nothing of what they may be in themselves," he, in turn, defines what he means by "objects of sense." They are "objects of experience" in the sense that nothing other than organized experiences are known.

The objects we know, according to Kant, are our experiences, which in no way inform of realities existing independent of our experiences. Mistaking features of experience for properties of a reality other than experience is consequently regarded as an "illusion," although in specifying which type of misinterpretation of experience is an "illusion," Kant himself employs the ambiguous term "object." He says, it is an "illusion" if "the intuition, by which an object is given us, is considered a concept of *the thing*."[6]

In distinguishing his philosophy from other philosophies, Kant uses terms which easily give rise to misunderstanding. The terms, however, which he uses, it must be acknowledged, are not ambiguous for him, or for anyone who keeps in mind the premise of his theory of knowledge—which is that no features of experience inform of realities other than experience. And when this premise is clearly understood, the term, "object," as well as the expression, "objects of experience," is unambiguous. Neither, however, can be understood within the scope of conventional definitions, because Kant does not use conventional language with conventional definitions. And this fact constitutes what he regards as "critical" philosophy.

If, however, terms are interpreted in their conventional senses, rather than in the senses given by Kant, no statement could be more misleading than, "We can know objects only as they *appear* to us."[7] A term such as "physical body" designates, according to Kant, what it does for anyone who thinks about a reality existing independent of experience. But a "physical body" as "a thing-in-itself" is not, according to Kant, an object of knowledge.[8] Although Kant does not doubt its existence, he denies that any aspect of its nature is knowable in experience, or by means of experience.

In order to understand critical terms in philosophies of knowledge, one must understand the basic premises of such philosophies, since the expanded senses with which words are used in premises of philosophies are themselves philosophies. The critical terms, therefore, "body," "object," and expressions such as "object of experience" and "object of sense," are defined within a philosophy by the premise of the philosophy itself. Everyone who reflectively uses language has some philosophy, since his reflecting is his philosophy. The most common terms used in philosophies such as "object," "body," "object of experience," consequently, cannot be taken for

28

granted. Understanding each one of these terms or expressions is itself a philosophical achievement. A clearly formulated analysis of the meaning of so commonly used an expression as "a matter of fact" is itself a philosophy. Hence Locke does not resolve any problem when he says: "He that would not deceive himself ought to build his hypothesis on *matter of fact*."[9] He rather states a problem. It is ascertaining the meaning of the expression, "matter of fact."

Experiences are often characterized as "immediate," and yet, this term itself is ambiguous. Its ambiguity, in fact, is so pervasive in philosophies that it is almost impossible to understand the point of view expressed by means of it. Anyone, irrespective of his theory of knowledge, for example, might say, as Professor Whitehead does, that "presentational immediacy is that peculiar way in which contemporary things are 'objectively' in our experience."[10] Hume could say this. So could Locke. So could Kant. Yet, in each of their affirmations, the expression, "contemporary things," would have different meanings. The ambiguity with which Professor Whitehead himself uses the expression, "presentational immediacy," becomes apparent when he says, "experience can predetermine to a considerable extent . . . characteristics of the presentational immediacy in succeeding moments of experience."[11] It is obvious, therefore, that if characteristics of an experience are conditioned, or "determined" by other experiences, they are not "presentationally immediate," since in so far as experiences are conditioned by other experiences, they are *mediated* by them.

An interpreting experience may be said to be immediate, but an interpreting experience includes many aspects of experience. It includes all that is designated as "remembering," "generalizing," "inferring," and any number of other activities. Since the conditioning of all experience is complex, the expression, "presentational immediacy" is thus actually nothing more than a vacuous literary flourish.

Another philosophically vacuous expression is "the moment's presentation" which occurs, for example, in Bradley's statement that phenomenalism must "keep to the moment's presentation, and must leave there the presented entirely as it is given." [12] Both the expressions, "the moment's presentation" and "the presented entirely as it is given," are ambiguous. As used in a so-called "direct realism" they refer to realities other than experience. In a form of idealism, or empiricism, such as Berkeley defends, they refer to experiences whose order is an expression of God's mind! Thus Berkeley's so-called "empiricism" as a theory of knowledge about the nature of "the immediately given" entails even a theology!

A reflective person should not speak of "immediate experience" or "immediate consciousness" of a reality of whose nature he can be informed only by mediating means. No astronomer, for example, has "immediate consciousness" of heavenly bodies. His knowledge of their nature is mediated by all that he does in taking advantage of the equipment comprising his "scientific method." Knowing anything about the nature of God is likewise mediated by all that is instrumental in enlightening men of His nature in relation to life and the world, and this includes the role of the sciences. One, consequently, must wonder what is meant in speaking, as Wobbermin does, about "the *immediacy* of fundamental religious experience." [13] After one has thought about all that is entailed in the expression, "revering God the Creator," he becomes aware that there is nothing in reflective religious life to which the expression, "immediate experience," or "immediate consciousness" refers. The expressions, "immediate consciousness," "a moment's presentation," "presentational immediate," are semantically vacuous in comparison with any rich experience affirming a religious faith that "The Heavens declare His glory."

30

2. *Sensory experiences are not knowledge*

Even the elementary term "sensation" is ambiguous as it is used in theories of knowledge. By this term, for example, Locke means "sens*ed* content," whereas Berkeley means "sens*ing*." According to Locke, qualities of physical realities supply the content for at least some experiences. Berkeley, however, denies this possibility. According to him, sensing is sensed content; and, conversely, sensed content is sens*ing*. He, therefore, does not distinguish between sensing and sensed content as Locke does, since, according to him, sensing experiences are "sensible" realities known in sensory experiences. Although both Locke and Berkeley regard themselves as empiricists, both use the critical terms of empiricism with very different meanings. Berkeley regards "sensa" as features of sensory experiences: whereas Locke regards at least some of them as qualities of physical reality other than experience.

If sensa are defined as exclusively sensory experiences, there obviously are no sensa apart from experience. Hence, when sensa are said to be "nothing but" experiences, as Berkeley maintains, it follows that there is no acquaintance with sensible features of a reality other than experience. But this follows only when the terms "sensa" and "sensory data" are defined consistently with the premise of a *radical* empiricist theory of knowledge.

There are many versions of empiricism. One version maintains that although there are realities other than experiences, nothing of their nature is disclosed in experiences. This point of view, however, may equally well be classified as a version of realism, since it affirms a duality of features of experience and properties of a reality other than experience. Hume's version of empiricism does not include this dualistic premise, since Hume does not contrast what is known with what is not known. He is preoccupied with what is knowable, and,

31

according to him, this is sensory experience interpreted as sensory experience. Kant, on the other hand, makes the distinction between experiences and realities other than experiences because his philosophy of knowledge presupposes the metaphysic that there are realities other than experience, of whose nature, however, *nothing* is known in experience.

In criticism of Hume's consistent version of the extreme empiricist premise, it must be pointed out that sensations are particular; and, as such, cannot be known, since every knowing experience is also an interpreting experience—and such interpreting experiences are not sensory experiences. Speaking about knowledge exclusively in terms of sensory experiences is, consequently, misleading, since even an awareness of sensory experiences includes more than sensory experiences.

This distinction between sensations as experiences and sensations as "objects of knowledge" is made by Aristotle when he declares, "None of our sense perceptions is wisdom, though it is they which give us the most assured knowledge of individual facts." [14] A sensation is a type of experience; and an interpretation of its informative significance is another type of experience. Since interpretations of sensations may be mistaken, judgments about their informative role may also be mistaken. According to Aristotle, there is no error in sensations, but only in interpretations of sensations; and sensations are *erroneously interpreted* when they are assumed to be informative of a reality of which there is no "sens*ed* content."

It is obvious from the foregoing analysis that the term "sensation" is used both with the sense of sign-experience which refers beyond itself, and also with the sense of experience which does not refer beyond itself. When, therefore, one affirms he "has a sensation," it is impossible to know his intended meaning. But when one declares that he has a "sensation *of*" something, the preposition, "of," refers beyond

32

sensation itself. Although this sign-function is "obvious" for all who assume a reality to which sensations refer, it is not equally "obvious" for those who do not assume this.

Everyone acknowledges that sensations are experiences; but some who formulate philosophies about the nature of knowledge do not believe that sensations inform of realities other than themselves. A condition for survival, however, is the capacity for taking account of realities to which sensations refer. An elementary fact, therefore, of which account must be taken in philosophies, is the common practice of interpreting some sensations as signs. And philosophies which repudiate this type of interpretation of practice do so on the grounds of a premise that does not take into account all of the data to which reflective attention logically may, and practically must, be directed. One consequently cannot help being impressed with their arbitrary procedure. A philosophy which interprets adjustment behavior, however, cannot ignore conditions essential for such behavior, and one such condition is regarding at least some sensations as informative of physical realities. A reality to which sensations are believed to refer is regarded in common practice as "sensed"; and the features of sensation are regarded as sensed properties. Kant dismisses this analysis as "naive," maintaining that "Things as objects of our senses existing outside us are given, but we know *nothing* of what they may be in themselves."[15] Yet, the sole basis for regarding it as "naive" is that it is at variance with his dogmatic dualistic premise.

The premise of his so-called "critical" philosophy, however, dismisses as unsound only one point of view affirmed in common practice. It is that sensations are informative of "sensible" features of reality other than experience. But it takes for granted the premise of common practice that sensations do refer beyond themselves. In regarding some sensations as referring to realities other than experiences, Kant assumes that common practice is justified in believing in the sign-function

33

of sensations, but he denies that sensations *inform* of such realities, for he insists that "the constitution of our sensibility" alone is known in analyzing sensory experiences. He regards as sound the point of view affirmed in common practice that there is a reality other than "our sensibilities," and maintains that "The constitution of our sensibility . . . is specifically affected by (such) objects." But of the nature of such objects, he declares, we know nothing: "Objects . . . are in themselves unknown."[16]

Although Kant takes for granted that it is a fact that some adjustments are effective for survival, his theory of knowledge, nevertheless, is incapable of accounting for this fact because he does not respect the soundness of the basic cognitive presumption in common practice. Locke, on the other hand, respects the soundness of this presumption when he maintains that there is "knowledge of the existence" of things "by sensation."[17] In agreeing with Locke, however, it must be urged that the nature of the physical world is not known only by means of sensation, although sensations are included in the data by means of which its nature is interpreted, and by means of which it may in part be known.

3. *Knowledge is not only of perceptions*

The term "perception," or its equivalent, is always included in vocabularies of philosophies about the nature of knowledge, but the meanings with which this term is used vary with philosophies. A philosophy, for example, whose basic premise is that experiences alone are knowable uses this term interchangeably with "perceiving"; and when perceiving is regarded as the reality of which knowledge is claimed, the term "perceiving" is used with fundamentally the same meaning as the term "sensing." When, however, the term "sensing" is distinguished from the term "sensed," a comparable distinction is carried over into the correlated terms "perceiving" and

34

"perceived." Distinguishing between "sensing" and "perceiving" as experiences is, however, of minor significance in a philosophy about the nature of knowledge; whereas specifying the type of reality *of which* there are such experiences is stating the basic premise of a theory of knowledge.

Such a procedure of stipulating the range of realities referred to by a term is itself a contribution to knowledge; and it is this type of knowledge alone which is the significant achievement in *a philosophical analysis* of the nature of knowledge. In declaring, for example, that "Perception is a mental event," the nature of perception is understood no more than is the nature of "mental event." Yet, defining perception as "mental" clarifies the *type* of reality to which both terms are referred. So likewise, understanding that the aspect of life to which we refer as "perceiving" is one element in what we designate as "mental" is an instructive classification. It enables us to understand, as Russell points out, that "properly speaking it is not the eye that sees: it is the brain, or the mind."[18]

When, therefore, one understands that there is no perception of any reality which is not also an interpretation, he becomes aware of the profound significance of Descartes' insistence that "bodies themselves are not properly perceived by the senses . . . but by the intellect."[19] Yet, in speaking about perceptions in terms of intellect, one should not assume that he thereby understands the nature of perception, since in this language-procedure he understands only a classification. Naming one type of experience "sensation"; another "perception"; and another "idea," is certainly not comprehending the complexity of any of them—although in associating informed distinctions with these terms, these terms are informative of distinctions in experiences.

4. *Knowledge is not only of phenomena*

Every experience of which we are aware is formed; and although this may be admitted by anyone who analyzes experiences, analyses of the nature of such form are as diverse as are theories of knowledge. It is not even pressing a point too much to maintain that the fundamental difference in theories of knowledge is the view taken about the nature of *formed* experiences. A theory of knowledge, for example, which maintains that only experiences are knowable must necessarily also maintain that the organization of experiences can be understood exclusively in terms of experiences. Although Kant maintains that organized experiences, or phenomena, are known, he nevertheless maintains that they are organized by capacities which are not features of experiences. According to him, an "object of experience" is an interpreted experience; and as such, it is a *formed* experience. It is not a physical reality, but an "appearance."

The affirmation, however, that we know only "an appearance of this physical world" is ambiguous, since the "world" to which Kant refers in his theory of knowledge is not the "world" of which he thinks as a scientist. Although he does not doubt that physical realities exist independent of experience, he maintains that what is known of them is limited to experience. What, therefore, is ambiguous is the term "world," since the "world" which is *known* as an "object of experience" consists, according to Kant, of experiences formed by the subject, and *in no way* corresponds to features or properties of the physical world.

Kant's distinction between the "world which exists" and the "world which is known" is unqualified; and when this unqualified dualistic premise is kept in mind, there is no justifiable basis for misunderstanding his philosophy. But when this dualistic premise is not constantly kept in mind, terms such as "appearance" and "representation" are misconstrued because they admit of more than one meaning. The term "world," as used by Kant, has two radically different meanings. As object of knowledge, it is phenomena; and as a reality existing independent of experience, it is noumena. Phenomena and noumena are radically different, or as Russell says in commenting on a radical dualistic theory of knowledge: "The one thing we know about the world is that it is not what it seems!"

The expression, "our interpretations of the world," is, therefore, ambiguous for anyone who reads Kant's philosophy with a vocabulary which is not defined exactly as Kant defines it. Kant's vocabulary is, consequently, disturbing because it consists of language used in common practice after it has been divested of every sense with which it is used in such practice. The expression, likewise, "perception of actual objects," is disturbing because ambiguous. Its ambiguity, however, can be removed by speaking about "experienced objects as *consisting of experiences,*" and this is the meaning with which Kant uses the expression, "objects . . . as they appear to us."[20] Objects which "appear to us" are, according to him, interpreted *experiences,* and are not realities other than experiences.

It must be pointed out that the term "appearance" has one, and only one, meaning in Kant's philosophy, although it is used with various meanings in other philosophies. In some philosophies, it is used with the sense of "fragmentary or partial reality"; and when so used, it is assumed that there is a reality other than experience, some of whose features "appear" in experience. Alexander, for example, uses the term "appearance" with this sense when he speaks of appearances as "partial revelations to the mind" of a reality existing independent of a mind.[21] The "appearance of things," according to Kant, on the other hand, is "never their constitution in themselves."[22] In understanding, therefore, what Kant means by the expression, "things in themselves," one understands also what Kant means by "objects of knowledge" as "*mere* appearances."

37

The expression "things in themselves," however, is confusing since it often has a meaning in a metaphysic which it does not have in a theory of knowledge. A knowing experience is a relating activity; and knowledge is a type of relation in which a subject is informed about the nature of a reality which is the "object of his knowing." It thus is obvious that nothing is both "a thing in itself" and also "an object of knowledge," since in so far as anything is "an object of knowledge," it is related to a subject. The very knowing of an "object of knowledge" which is not in relation to a knowing subject is, therefore, contradictory; and so the expression, "thing in itself," is contradicted by the expression, "object of knowledge."

Every philosophy which uses a language borrowed from common practice, but divested of all its conventional senses, sooner or later faces the difficulty of ambiguity. But in attempting to remove such ambiguity, a philosopher often goes counter to the mentality of a people whose language he uses; as for example, when Kant declares that "objects which cannot be given us in any experience do not exist for us."[23] Stated in less involved language, it is: "Things we do not experience, we do not know!" This trivial meaning, however, is not the full significance of this statement, but it does, nevertheless, specify that any reality which is not included in our experiences is not a known reality—it "does not exist *for* us" in the sense that *we know nothing about it*. According to Kant, the physical world and every object in it fits this description, as well as a divine reality which is other than the world.

Kant's philosophy is a logically consistent expansion of a radical dualistic premise. Its logical consistency, however, is not a demonstration of the soundness, or the logical inescapability of the dualistic premise. In declaring, therefore, that "The phenomenality of the empirical world was made fully clear by Kant," Jaspers confuses the consistency of Kant's analysis of this premise with the soundness of the premise.[24]

Jaspers' affirmation would indeed be little more than obvious if it declared no more than the fact that Kant clearly analyzes the term "phenomena" or "phenomenality." His affirmation, however, means more than this. It means that Kant's theory of knowledge is philosophically cogent, and it is the soundness of this estimate which must be questioned.

Jaspers defends its soundness when he declares: "Whatever we know is only a beam of light cast by our interpretations."[25] Although there is no ambiguity in this analysis of the content of knowledge, a distinction must, nevertheless, be made between knowledge which consists of interpretations and knowledge which is exclusively of interpretations. *If* realities other than one's own experiences are knowable, interpretations of the nature of such realities may also comprise a content of knowledge. The conditional or hypothetical form of this statement, it must be pointed out, is simply an expression of caution in using language, and in no way is an expression of a lack of confidence in the existence of such a reality, or in the possibility of knowing it. According to Kant's dualistic premise, however, there is no such possibility of knowing the nature of a reality which exists independent of our experiences, since its nature and our interpretations of its nature are radically different. *If,* on the other hand, there is a reality to which we refer by the term "world," and *if* there is any aspect of its nature of which we have acquaintance, then neither Kant, nor anyone else, has made it "fully clear" that knowledge is *only* of phenomena.

According to the theory of knowledge defended in this study, the cognitive significance of experience is not an aspect entirely of a subject, but is rather a type of relation between a subject and a reality other than a subject. In knowing the meaning of an informed affirmation about such a reality, one would then be informed of two realities—a subject's interpretation; and a reality about which his interpretations inform him. The very possibility, however, that any interpretations may be enlightened of the nature of realities other than a subject's interpretations is denied by phenomenalistic philosophies, such as some modern philosophies of existence.

According to Marcel, for example, the motive of philosophy is knowing "not so much what reality is, as what *we mean* when we assert its existence." [26] Although this analysis of philosophy is clear, the meaning of the term "existence," however, is not equally clear, and its deep-rooted meaning in common language does not provide a clue for understanding its meaning in philosophies of existence. Marcel, on the other hand, specifies the *phenomenalistic* meaning of the term "existence" when he says: "What I wanted to know was not so much what reality is, as what *we mean* when we assert its existence."

Although delimiting the range of philosophy to the restricted scope of phenomenalism is an understandable procedure, formulating a philosophy of religion within the strictures of such a limitation is certainly questionable. And Jaspers illustrates this questionable procedure when he says: "Augustine's works remain to this day a spring from which all thinkers draw who seek *to know the soul* in its depths." [27] Although it must be acknowledged that this is one aspect of the significance of Augustine's writings, it must also be acknowledged that Augustine endeavored to know the nature of his life in relation to God, and this entailed for him taking account of all he understood in the nature of the world which he esteemed as God's creation. And in endeavoring to know the nature of God as a condition for knowing the nature of the world as God's creation, Augustine, therefore, endeavored to know a reality very different from his interpretations. Consistent with his primary interest in experiences, however,

40

Jaspers maintains: "What matters is not our knowledge of God, but our attitude towards God." [28] Although one must admit that this is an eminently important aspect of a philosophy of religion, he must, nevertheless, also insist that the aspect of religion which is of supreme importance to religious life itself is a knowledge of God, "the Lord who made all things." [29]

Chapter III

SUBJECTIVITY WITHOUT SUBJECTIVISM

1. *Subjectivity must be distinguished from subjectivism*

A frequently occurring fallacy is the generalizing of an entire philosophy from the fact that experience is conditioned by a subject. A subject is indeed a condition for experience; and this fact is the subjective aspect of all experience. But maintaining that this aspect of experience is the *exclusive* feature of experience is a fallacious generalization. Thinking, for instance, is an experience, but what is thought about is not necessarily a thinking experience. In confusing a thinking experience with thought as a pattern of mental experience, or with the content of such experience, and in maintaining that thought is exclusively an individual's experience, some philosophers conclude that thought has only features of particular experiences. When, however, thought is analyzed as a *pattern* of mental experience, it need not be regarded as purely subjective. It is subjective as occurring in a subject's experience, but it is not subjective in the sense that it is unique to a particular person's experience. Thus a subjectivism which maintains that ideas are exclusively subjective, in the sense that they are unique to each subject having them, rests upon what Bosanquet calls "a deep foundation of imperfect logic."[1]

Particular ideas are unique in so far as they are instances of a type of experience, but they are not unique in so far as they share features in common; and this distinction is assumed

42

by everyone who speaks of "his" ideas in contrast to another's ideas. Communicating between two persons is, in fact, possible only because one's own ideas are not exclusively *his* own. Thus, whereas an individual's ideas are "his" in one sense, they are not "his" in another sense; and this ambiguity is basic to subjectivistic philosophies. In so far as one communicates with another, he is partially informed of the nature of another's ideas. And when this is denied, it is not a consequence of observing, but of the dogmatic premise of philosophical subjectivism.

The subjective conditioning of experience is an empirical fact, since, as Professor Whitehead points out, "you cannot retreat from mere subjectivity; for subjectivity is what we carry with us." [2] Subjectivism, on the other hand, is a dogmatic philosophy, and as a philosophy, it is a set of affirmations exemplifying one use of language. But the language used in affirming a philosophy is anything but "subjective" as this term is used in philosophical subjectivisms. No language used in communicating is exclusively an individual's own. In selecting a language, an individual selects from others' property; and he uses their property with meanings which they in part give. In using words with meanings which are unique to one's own vocabulary, on the other hand, an individual invents a language. But inventing a language which one alone understands is not communicating. It is engaging in soliloquy. Russell thus points out a significant fact about the use of language when he says that "what is most personal in each individual's experience tends to evaporate during the process of translation into language." [3]

If a person were to know only his own language, he could not even understand the language with which others affirm their points of view. Hence any evaluation he would make of the unsoundness of the view of others would only be a judgment upon *his own view,* since he could know only his own view. But he could not even sensibly evaluate his own

43

philosophy as superior to other philosophies without presuming to understand *them*. An evaluation, furthermore, of a philosophy as sounder than others is meaningful only in comparison with some criterion, and yet, a criterion by which a subjectivism is evaluated as "sounder" than other philosophies cannot itself be a subjectivism, otherwise subjectivism would have to affirm itself as a normative philosophy. There is, however, no proponent of subjectivism who would willingly be entrapped in this presumption, since a denial that there are norms which are knowable is a basic premise of subjectivism as a consistent philosophy. Any criterion by which an evaluation "sound" could sensibly be affirmed of any philosophy would have to be other than the philosophy itself; and yet, it is just such a criterion, according to a subjectivism, which is not knowable. One defending subjectivism, consequently, is in the strange dilemma of knowing that his philosophy is sound without also knowing any standard by which it is sound!

An individual defending a philosophical subjectivism certainly would be inconsistent with his own point of view if he affirmed his philosophy for the specific purpose of enlightening another person; and it was this inconsistency which impressed Socrates. Protagoras, for example, affirmed the premise of subjectivism, and yet saw nothing inconsistent in presuming to be a better teacher than others on the ground that he defended a philosophy which was sounder than all other philosophies. Socrates, however, pointed out that in going to Protagoras for the purpose of learning his philosophy, men reveal their disbelief of its very soundness, for "In all these instances, men themselves believe that wisdom and ignorance exist in the world of men." [4]

The confidence itself with which a person defends subjectivism as sound cannot be justified by subjectivism, since in defending subjectivism as a sound point of view, subjectivists do not argue that it is sound only for them. Yet, saying that it is sound, but not only for them, they presume to know something about its character as intellectually compelling for all who reflect. As Brunner points out, subjectivism as a philosophy thus presents a "comic contrast to the confidence with which these philosophers champion—and demonstrate —their theory as 'correct,' i.e., universally valid!"[5]

If a subjectivist were consistent, he would believe as Gorgias did, although he would not affirm his belief as Gorgias did. As the most profound of the ancient Sophists, Gorgias acknowledged that "if perchance a man should come to know (something), it would remain a secret, (for) he would be unable to describe it to his fellow-men."[6]

2. *Epistemological subjectivism must be distinguished from methodological subjectivism*

Knowledge would be confined exclusively to a person's own experiences if *all* his ideas were constructed out of experiences *unique* to himself. Many philosophers, however, are not satisfied with this type of subjectivism as a theory of knowledge, and consequently classify this process of constructing ideas as "methodological," by which they mean that *the process of constructing ideas* begins with a person's own experiences. When this distinction, therefore, is made between the process of constructing ideas and the knowledge significance of ideas, methodological subjectivism may be respected as a sound empirical analysis of the *genesis* of ideas. A methodology, however, passes into an epistemology when an analysis of the genesis of ideas includes an interpretation of what is known by means of ideas. And this transition is so easily made that it is understandable how methods of analyzing ideas pass from an analytical procedure into a dogma about the nature of what is known.

An individual's ideas are constructions formed in the course of his experiences; and in maintaining no more than this,

45

one restricts his analysis of ideas to an empirical method. In pointing out that ideas develop from "first person" experiences, nothing more, therefore, is maintained than that an individual's ideas are his own experiences. And anyone, irrespective of his theory of knowledge, might maintain this. Subjectivistic empiricism as a theory of knowledge, however, is not implied in such an empirical methodology; and it is not implied for the very reason that a methodology is an analysis of method, whereas a theory of knowledge is an analysis of what is known, or is believed known, by means of particular methods. Since, however, an empirical methodology is so often confused with an empiricist theory of knowledge, a distinction between a method of analysis and an interpretation of the nature of knowledge must carefully be stressed.

A person is not the only significant factor in forming ideas, or in constructing concepts. Yet, in so far as the role of a person is stressed as alone significant, a theory of knowledge is taken for granted; and an exclusive emphasis upon a subject, rather than upon a reality to which a subject is related, is a solipsism which stresses the self-centered character of experience. This so-called "self-centered" character of experience is often regarded as the "ego-centric predicament." Yet, the only person who thinks of such a so-called "predicament" is he who thinks of every feature of his experiences as unique to himself, and not as his responses to realities other than his experiences.

When, on the other hand, realities other than experience are regarded as "experienced," one does not think of his ideas as "first person" experiences, but as interpretations of realities which are other than his experiences. Or, in order to avoid any interpretation constituting a subjectivistic solipsism, it would be better to say that any reality interpreted by a person is at least one factor which must be taken into account in analyzing a person's ideas about such a reality. And when this

46

procedure is followed, one does not stress "reality as it is for a subject." He stresses rather a subject's responses to a reality other than a subject as means for interpreting *its* nature— although, of course, interpreting its nature is by means of his ideas. A "methodological solipsism" as a theory of procedure, therefore, should not be confused with solipsism as a theory of knowledge. When reflecting upon experiences, however, is regarded as the *only* method for acquiring knowledge, an empirical procedure is interpreted from the point of view of empiricism as a subjectivistic theory of knowledge. And when the point of view of such an empiricism is taken for granted, a "methodological solipsism" becomes equivalent to solipsism as a version of consistent subjectivism. Regarding a subject and his experiences as the only realities which are knowable, however, is not a consequence of a methodology, or method of analysis, but is rather implied in the premise of a theory of knowledge which is taken for granted when one employs a method of analysis.

Individuals who adjust to the context in which they endeavor to survive do not think of "for me entities." They think of such things only after they have philosophized, and their philosophy has clamped strictures upon their interpretations of their experiences. Unreflected upon experiences *in adjustment behaviors* are specifically "object centered," and the type of object which is the focus of such rudimentary behavior is other than experience. The "data of experience" in adjustment behaviors are construed as reports of realities other than experience, and it is such realities reported in experience which impress individuals who seriously endeavor to make effective adjustments. When at least some experiences are regarded as responses to realities other than experience, then at least some experiences are interpreted in terms of realities other than experiences. Hence, as Schlick points out, becoming aware that "primitive experience is not first-person experience (is) one of the most important steps which philosophy must take towards the clarification of its deepest problems."[7]

Analyzing experiences is a procedure, or an empirical method. Such an analysis need not, however, take the premise of subjectivistic empiricism for granted; and when it does not take it for granted, an empirical analysis of experience may well include statements about "ideas of reality other than experience"—some of which *may* be informed of such realities. One reflects upon statements in analyzing what is *said* about realities other than experience, and the analysis of such statements is empirical, although the statements so analyzed are not about statements, but about realities other than statements. Merely acknowledging the *possibility* for such informed ideas is affirming an alternative to *subjectivistic* empiricisms which affirm the "ego-centric predicament" as the only fact of significance in interpreting experiences.

Defending an ego-centric philosophy, which maintains that an individual's own experiences constitute the exclusive scope of knowledge for him, involves a disregard for ordinary syntax, since in speaking about "one's own" experiences, an individual assumes that he distinguishes them from another person's experiences. An individual's use of the qualifier "my" or "mine" would, in fact, be meaningless if he were to assume that he is acquainted only with his own experiences. The term "my" in common usage is meaningful only when thought of in contrast to something which is acknowledged as other than one's own. But when anything other than one's own cannot even *in principle* be acknowledged, one misuses the qualifier "my" or "mine." Thus in maintaining that experiences alone are knowable, one could not seriously speak of his own experiences as "mine," since the sole sense of "mine" in language—which is social—is in contrast to what is not one's own. And yet, any reality other than one's own cannot be acknowledged by a consistent ego-centric philosophy.

Affirmations about one's own perspective or experiences,

48

however, would not even be reports of his own perspective or experiences if they were not in ego-centric language, and consequently, ego-centric terms such as "I," "mine," "this," "here," "now," are admissible in any sensible person's vocabulary. Admitting them into a vocabulary, however, is one thing. Using them as the *only* vocabulary is something very different. Yet, it is this thoroughly arbitrary usage which is basic to all consistent ego-centric philosophies. The "predicament" of such philosophies is, therefore, only their biased vocabulary. And this is self-imposed. It certainly is not imposed by any so-called "facts of experience." Only one fact of experience accounts for it. It is the arbitrary delimiting of the rich vocabulary of reflective life to the strictures of a few words which stress the *sole* significance of the self in *all* its experiences.

Ego-centric terms, as a matter of fact, can easily be eliminated from one's vocabulary. "Here," for example, may be replaced by a statement in terms of latitude and longitude. The term "now" may be replaced by a date. In thus using terms which do not include reference to a subject, but refer to a reality other than a subject, an "object language" emerges such as is used in the physical sciences and in daily discourse.

3. *The subjective conditioning of knowing must be distinguished from knowledge*

Locke's statement, "All our knowledge consist(s) in the view the mind has of its own ideas" is either ambiguous or inaccurate; and its ambiguity or inaccuracy is due to confusing a procedure in analyzing the origin of ideas with an analysis of knowledge which is confined exclusively to ideas.[8] Everyone, irrespective of his philosophy, would agree with Locke that one aspect of knowledge consists "in the view the mind has of its own ideas," but relatively few would maintain that knowledge is *confined* to ideas.

One aspect of knowledge is an awareness of ideas; and

Locke stresses this fact in declaring that knowledge is the "view the mind has of the agreement and disagreement of its ideas, or of the relation they have one to another."[9] In maintaining this, however, he does not also maintain that the scope of knowledge is limited to *ideas of relations between ideas.* He maintains rather that at least some ideas are informed interpretations of realities other than ideas; and so in saying that "our knowledge consists in the perception of the agreement or disagreement of any two ideas," he understates the extent of knowledge which he himself believes is possible.[10] In so doing, he thus confuses ideas as the only realities which are knowable with ideas as means for knowing realities other than ideas; and this confusion is apparent in his assertion: "Our knowledge is founded on and employed about our ideas only."[11]

Everyone would maintain that knowledge is "founded" on ideas, but only subjectivistic empiricists maintain that knowledge is "about our ideas only." In understanding a description of a "physical reality," for example, one knows ideas; but if ideas are all that is knowable, the adjective "physical" is misleading, because ambiguous. The term "physical" is used both for classifying descriptions, and also for describing realities existing independent of descriptions. Hence a single sense of the term "physical" should not be taken for granted in philosophies about the nature of knowledge, but must be explicitly indicated. A subjectivistic empiricism construes "knowledge of the physical" as knowledge of ideas, and Schlick *seems* to defend this analysis when he declares: "The adjectives 'physical' and 'mental' formulate only two different representational modes by which the data of experience are ordered; they are different ways of *describing* reality."[12] What is thus confusing in Schlick's statement is the term "reality," since a reality described as "physical" is ordinarily assumed to be other than experience. Yet, if the only realities believed to be knowable are "modes by which the data of experience

50

are ordered," it follows that knowledge must be analyzed exclusively in terms of ideas. According to this analysis, modes for ordering "the data of experience" are ideas; and in knowing a "physical" mode for ordering experience, one knows only a type of experience.

Ideas, however, are both means for knowing realities other than ideas, and are also themselves objects of knowledge. In distinguishing these two roles of ideas, one, therefore, distinguishes a theory of knowledge which maintains that knowing is an awareness only of ideas from another theory which regards ideas as a means for knowing realities which may be other than ideas.

For instance, in the physical sciences many ideas are proposed as hypotheses for interpreting realities believed to be observed, and so are believed to be other than ideas. Chromatin, for example, is a material in the nucleus of a cell which is observable by means of a microscope. Previous to cell division, it separates into small bodies called chromosomes, which are believed to be physical bases for heredity. Since, however, the number of observable chromosomes is relatively small, it is assumed that each in turn consists of many factors for determining heredity, although these additional factors are not observed. This assumption is called the genes hypothesis. Genes are not observed, but hereditarily determined features of living bodies are observed, whose great number is accounted for by the genes hypothesis. The genes hypothesis is thus a complex idea proposed for interpreting non-ideational realities believed to be physical determinants of heredity. The idea of genes is thus empirically significant because it enables biologists to interpret what they observe —or what they believe they observe.

Another example of ideas proposed for interpreting the nature of realities other than ideas may be cited from astronomy. An idea about the temperature of the sun, for example, is not an analysis of an idea. It is rather an interpretation of

51

the nature of the physical sun. No feature of an idea of the sun, for instance, is interpreted in terms of temperatures "of the order of 20 million degrees" as the sun itself is interpreted.[13] In affirming that "the sun is delivering heat and light . . . into space at a rate of 72,000 horsepower for every square yard of its surface," one interprets the sun—not his ideas about the sun or his visual images of the sun.[14]

If one's ideas about the sun are *informed* of the nature of the sun, his ideas are knowledge *of the sun;* and in interpreting affirmations of such ideas, he has knowledge of true statements about the sun. Understanding true statements about the sun is thus knowing more than affirmed ideas or statements. It is knowing the nature of the sun as its nature is interpreted in the meaning of statements. Interpreting statements may thus be a means for knowing ideas affirmed in statements as well as for knowing something of the nature of a reality interpreted by such ideas.

Believing that there are realities to which some experiences refer is not primarily interpreting experiences, but is interpreting realities to which such experiences are believed to refer. A belief in the existence of realities other than experience is, therefore, an inference from experience only when experiences are themselves interpreted as reporting such realities. What is believed to be known of realities other than experiences is indeed in terms of experience; yet, experiences are regarded as informing of such realities only when the premise is taken for granted that there are realities other than experiences, some of whose properties are knowable by means of experiences.

An experience is regarded as a *perception* only when it is believed to refer to a reality of which it presumably informs. J. S. Mill soundly observes that experiences "are of no importance or interest to us except as marks from which we infer something beyond them." In affirming this, however, he acknowledges that experiences are regarded as perceptual signs only when it is taken for granted that there is a reality to which they refer; and he explicitly points this out when he says: "It is not the colour which is important to us, but the object of which those visible appearances testify the presence."[15] According to this analysis, experiences would not even be classified as "perceptions" unless they were regarded as referring to realities other than themselves.

4. *A reality other than experience is taken for granted*

The basic premise of a consistent subjectivistic empiricism is that no experiences inform of realities independent of experience. Knowing this much is, of course, presuming knowledge not only of experiences, but also of the soundness of the premise. And if a subjectivist were to assume that he knows nothing except experience, he would have no criterion by which he could ascertain that *affirmations* about realities other than experiences are false. On grounds of logical consistency alone, therefore, a thoroughgoing subjectivist cannot even consider the problem of the truth or falsity of affirmations themselves, since affirmations about affirmations must confront him with the same logical problem as affirmations about realities other than experience. Whatever the particular usage may be in speaking about truth or falsity, the terms "true" and "false" are always used in reference to some criterion, and no interpretation can sensibly be said to be true except as it is compared with something other than itself.

A belief which is informed of the nature of an interpreted reality is true; and its truth is a feature of an interpretation— not of an experience of interpreting. Interpreting is having beliefs; and the having of beliefs is a type of experience. But the basis for classifying experiences as true beliefs is their presumed reference to interpreted realities of whose nature they are believed to be informed. Although an interpretation regarded as true easily becomes a norm by which other

53

interpretations are regarded as erroneous, the classification "true" itself constitutes a much more perplexing problem than the classification "erroneous" or "false." Any interpretation may be regarded as false when compared with another which is regarded as true—this is merely a matter of comparing or contrasting one point of view with another. But when an interpretation is dismissed as false, it is taken for granted that another interpretation is true. The basis, however, for presuming the truth of such an interpretation is very different from the basis for regarding an interpretation as false according to the criterion of the presumed truth of another interpretation.

Rejecting interpretations as false when they are contradictory of interpretations regarded as true is a matter of a logical convention, and this is merely a matter of conforming to an elementary procedure stipulated by a rule of logic. Presuming, however, to know which interpretations are informed is not a matter of logic, but is a metalogical presumption, which is not sufficiently acknowledged in philosophies by virtue of the fact that most philosophers begin their reflecting with some beliefs which they assume to be true. Kant, for example, presumes no knowledge of realities existing independent of experience, although he takes for granted that there are such realities. Thus his philosophical reflecting is not detached from the most elementary of all beliefs, even though no part of his philosophy is devoted to justifying this belief. Like most everyone else, he presumes this belief is justified, and so says, "it never came into my head to doubt it." [16] Locke likewise regards the belief that there are physical realities existing independent of experience as an "assurance" which "deserves the name of knowledge"; and he does so only because he assumes there are realities by virtue of whose existence he presumes that this belief itself is true.

Before a person formulates a philosophy, he assumes that some of his beliefs are true; and the beliefs which he regards

54

as true are the ones he considers as worthy of being included in a philosophy. This procedure is compatible with sound philosophizing, however, only if such beliefs are acknowledged as initial assumptions. One aspect of philosophical reflecting, therefore, should be a specification of beliefs accepted with "assurance," or assumed to be true.

An assumption of all so-called "realistic" philosophies of knowledge is that there are realities other than experience, although only some versions of realism maintain that properties of such realities are knowable by means of experience. Those versions of realism which presume this, however, are faced with grave problems, one of which arises from the fact that a nerve fiber responds in one way to any stimulus which excites it, irrespective of the character of the stimulating body. In other words, a nerve has one and only one way of responding provided its stimulation is of sufficient strength and duration to excite it into activity. Thus a stimulation sufficient for exciting a nerve brings about a response peculiar to the nerve rather than to the stimulating body. Just how experiences can be informative of realities other than experiences, and so be effectively selective when nervous responses are not selective, is certainly a troublesome problem; and an awareness of this problem is acknowledged in insisting that "We have no power of penetrating to the object itself." Yet, affirming this much about experience, on the other hand, is presuming extensive knowledge of the nature not only of experience, but also of realities other than experience.

Locke, for instance, distinguishes a belief that there are realities other than experienc from whatever is thought about their properties. "Our idea of substance," he declares, "has no other idea of it at all, but only a supposition of (a) . . . support of such qualities which are capable of producing simple ideas in us." [17] He thus defends a dualistic version of realism in maintaining that there are two fundamentally different types of experiences—one which informs of a reality

55

existing independent of experience, and another which does not. According to this dualistic point of view, experiences are classified as "primary" if they are presumed to inform of such realities, and they are said to occur in a type of relation called "resemblance"; whereas features of experience which are not presumed to "resemble" properties of realities other than experience are classified as "secondary." And such secondary properties are said to be only *"thought* resemblances," but not real resemblances.[18]

One may assume, as Locke does, that some experiences inform of some properties of realities other than experience, and yet be aware of the purely verbal character of Locke's classification. Classifying experiences which are believed to inform of realities other than experience as "primary," and classifying experiences which are not believed to so inform as "secondary," is perfectly clear. But what is actually clear are only classifications and definitions of classificatory terms.

Locke, however, presupposes a knowledge of realities other than experience when he maintains that some qualities of experiences "are nothing in the objects themselves"; and what he assumes about their nature becomes the criterion by which he classifies experiences as "secondary."

Affirming that some experiences are informed of properties of physical reality, whereas others are not, is not an empirical procedure, as Berkeley pointed out, and is not consistent with an empiricist theory of knowledge. Locke dogmatically maintains: "Yellowness is not actually in gold," although there is "a power in gold to produce that idea in us by our eyes, when placed in a due light."[19] According to this analysis, color is peculiar to a perceptual *relation*, and is a feature of experience rather than of a physical object. Yet, a moment's reflection upon this *analysis* enables one to become aware of its arbitrary character, since all sensory data are equally experience. It is, consequently, arbitrary to maintain that

56

bodies have "bulk, figure, and texture" as reported by sensory experiences, whereas they have no property identifiable as color. The basis for making this distinction is a presumption —not an examination of experience itself—since so-called primary qualities of experience are also features of experience, although in relation to bodies presumed to be other than experience. Locke, nevertheless, regards this dichotomous classification as "critical"—just as everyone regards his own point of view as critical!

Everyone believes that he is critical of his own view, and for this reason maintains it with assurance. But being "critical" of one's own view includes a capacity for detecting arbitrary dogmatism in it; and this is one type of criticism which is difficult to achieve. It would, for example, be difficult for anyone who believes as Locke does to question the "critical" character of a premise maintaining a dualism between primary and secondary qualities; and it would be equally difficult for one who believes as Kant does to question the critical character of a thoroughgoing dualism between all experience and realities other than experience. Locke begins his reflecting on experience with a conviction that there is a duality *within* experience; and Kant begins his reflecting on experience with an equally strong conviction that there is a duality between experience and realities other than experience. Thus neither Locke nor Kant arrives at the premise of his own particular type of dualistic realism by analyzing experiences, since the dualistic presupposition peculiar to each is itself a premise on the basis of which each analyzes experience.

Locke classifies his version of realism as "critical" because he maintains a qualified dualism; and Kant classifies his version of realism as "critical" because he maintains an unqualified dualism. Thus realisms are euphemistically classified as "critical" which maintain both that *some* experiences inform of realities other than experiences, and also that *no* experiences inform of any reality existing independent of experience. Every philosophy may well be regarded as "critical" by someone; and when it is so regarded, it is looked upon by him as the norm by which other philosophies must be evaluated for their "critical" character.

5. *Every theory of knowledge is based upon assumptions*

Every philosophy includes assumptions whose dialectical defense is subsequent to their acceptance as sound. Accepting an assumption as sound is committing oneself to it; and such commitment is included in every philosophical defense of beliefs, notwithstanding the circular character of this procedure. But beliefs defended in reasoned arguments are regarded as sound apart from the arguments stated in defense of their soundness. Locke, for example, defends his conviction that some ideas, called "primary," are "the resemblances of something really existing in the objects themselves" as a premise in his philosophy because he regards it as sound; and every argument he offers in support of this conviction is included in his philosophy because he assumes some properties of physical objects, called "primary," are known.[20]

The particular term "primary," however, by which Locke classifies properties of realities other than experience is of no fundamental philosophical significance. But what is of fundamental philosophical significance is the *meaning* of this term—which is an interpretation of the status of properties presumed to be other than experience. In maintaining that physical realities which exist independent of experience exemplify properties of "solidity, extension, figure, number, and motion or rest," Locke both defines the *term* "physical realities" and also states a *proposition* about such realities. A definition of the term "primary" in Locke's philosophy, therefore, is not arbitrary, since it is actually a presumed analysis of the

58

nature of realities existing independent of being experienced.

The presumption that some properties of a reality other than experience are knowable is logically more fundamental in a theory of knowledge than is a specification of which particular properties are knowable. Hence in questioning the soundness of any particular analysis of properties of a reality existing independent of experience, one does not necessarily question the soundness of the presumption that there are realities having a status independent of experience, *some* of whose properties may be knowable. But if a theory of knowledge affirms that there is one and only one property of such a reality which is knowable, it must also specify what that property is. If, on the other hand, a theory of knowledge affirms only that *some* properties of realities other than experience may be knowable, it need not specify which these properties are. Although this distinction may be regarded as betraying a halfhearted sort of attitude, it is, nevertheless, a step in cautiously formulating a defensible theory of knowledge.

Believing that a reality other than experience may be knowable is not necessarily presuming that one actually can characterize it. A sound characterization of it presupposes that it is knowable, whereas a conviction about its knowability does not presuppose that the conditions for knowing it have actually been fulfilled. One may understand how conditions for knowing a reality may be fulfilled, and yet not fulfil such conditions; whereas fulfilling conditions for knowing a reality is knowing the reality to the extent of having fulfilled such conditions.

Everyone acquainted with modern scientific research is impressed with the complex nature of techniques for achieving reports of realities whose natures are investigated. Yet, the very assumption itself that there are such realities is far more complex than laboratory equipment. And although laboratory conditions for achieving a body of information in science are always clearly specified, the complexity of beliefs involved in ascertaining these conditions is seldom even partially specified. Another way of saying this is that our sciences, like our philosophies—like most of our lives—rest upon complex beliefs which are taken for granted.

Although we are aware of the complexity of some theories about the nature of the physical world, we are not equally aware of the complexity of beliefs we take for granted in affirming these theories. If we were, we should understand that we take far more for granted in our most learned analyses than we explicitly acknowledge. Few people, for example, presume to comment on the concept of simultaneity as analyzed by Albert Einstein. Yet, the late Professor Reichenbach points out that even this complex concept could conceivably enter into a body of beliefs which *everyone* might some day take for granted. And he specifies one condition on the basis of which this could conceivably occur: It would be establishing "a telephone connection with the planet Mars." If this were done, an inhabitant of the earth would soon learn that he had to "wait a quarter of an hour for the answer" to one of his questions. Professor Reichenbach then suggests that after having experiences such as this for a sufficiently long time, "the relativity of simultaneity would become as trivial a matter as the time difference between the standard times of different time zones is today." [21]

Types of experiences are named in philosophies, and steps in procedures are specified in scientific methodologies, but naming types of experiences and specifying procedures are not analyses of the complex assumptions themselves involved in such activities of naming and specifying procedures. Merely believing there is a reality, some of whose properties are knowable, is an assumption complex beyond all description in comparison with any "philosophical analysis" or procedure called "scientific method."

60

6. *The basic assumptions in theories of knowledge are not logically necessary*

An assumption that some experiences may be informed of properties of a reality other than experience is *logically* incompatible with an assumption which denies this. And in so far as each assumption is expanded into a philosophy, both philosophies are logically incompatible. But the logical incompatibility of two philosophies is no evidence that one is sound and the other is not. *If,* however, some experiences inform of realities other than experiences, a philosophy which defends the assumption that there are such experiences would then be sound. And it would be sound according to the criterion of performing an informative function. Although believing there are such experiences is a presumption which may be a premise of a philosophy, the presumption itself does not specify which particular experiences perform this informative role. A specific problem with which one is faced when he accepts this general presumption, therefore, is ascertaining which experiences perform this role. And endeavoring to ascertain which they are is the program of intelligent life. Included in this program are activities classified as scientific studies, philosophical reflections, and religious faith.

Interpreting features of experiences as informative of properties of realities other than experience, however, presumes knowledge both of experience and of realities other than experience. Such presumed knowledge is not a logical inference from any premise of a theory of knowledge: It is itself the premise of a theory of knowledge. Presuming such knowledge is the premise of some versions of realism; and the criterion of their soundness is their interpretation of the actual informative nature of experiences in relation to realities other than experience. When one takes for granted that there are such realities and that some experiences refer to them and report something of their nature, he also assumes the soundness of the basic premise of the version of realism defended by Locke, but repudiated by Hume and Kant.

In believing that a premise of a philosophy is sound, one also believes that a philosophy which is a consistent expansion of it is likewise sound. The circular character of this belief is not logically satisfying; and yet, it can be escaped only by an unequally unsatisfying dogmatism. In presuming, for example, that some experiences inform of realities other than themselves, one regards a particular interpretation of experience as sound; and when he selects features of experience as evidence for the soundness of this belief, he selects them according to the criterion of this very belief. Descartes recognized this troublesome fact when he acknowledged that even though sensory experiences have an involuntary character, he "did not think that (he) ought on that ground to conclude that they proceeded from things different from (him), since perhaps there might be found in (him) some faculty, though hitherto unknown to (him) which produced them." [22]

Although this caution expresses a reasonable type of procedure, it is, nevertheless, not a matter of logic, since a hesitancy in believing that there are realities other than experience is not motivated by logical considerations any more than affirming that there are realities is motivated by logical considerations. Affirming or denying that there are realities other than experience is not within the scope of logic, and so philosophies developed on the basis either of such affirming or of such denying may be equally logical.

The premise of a philosophy as such does not affect the logical character of a philosophy provided the premise is intelligible, and provided the philosophy is an expanded analysis of the premise. Hence in so far as an expansion of the premise of a philosophy is consistent with the premise, the philosophy itself is exempt from discrediting on logical grounds. One misunderstands the nature of logic, therefore, when he speaks of *logically* discrediting the premise of a philosophy. Although logically consistent deductions from the premise of a philosophy may enable one to detect its unsoundness, such deductions, on the other hand, do not themselves enable one to establish its soundness. Hume's philosophy, for example, is a logically consistent defense of the premise that no experiences inform of the nature of any reality other than experiences. Although logically coherent, its coherence as a philosophy does not establish the soundness of its basic premise.

In evaluating the soundness of the basic premise of any philosophy, a criterion other than logic must be considered. Hence even though a logical argument may be formulated in defense of Hume's premise, there is no *logical* means whatever for establishing its truth. The consistency of Hume's argument is a property of the expansion of his premise, but it is not a property of the premise. His belief that nothing can be known of a reality other than experience is simply his *interpretation* of the cognitive significance of experience. His philosophy is a splendid example of a logically coherent argument, consistent with the premise that we learn nothing in experience about the nature of realities other than experience. But his philosophy, no more than any other of its type, cannot logically discredit the soundness of an alternative premise that some experiences may inform of realities other than experience.

Philosophies of the type formulated by Hume lend reasoned support to their basic premise. But the reasoned support of a premise is not conclusive evidence for its soundness, since any intelligible premise may be defended coherently in a philosophy. Both Hume's premise and its denial cannot, of course, be defended in one philosophy, although they may both be defended as philosophies. One affirms that some experiences inform of realities other than experience, whereas the other denies this; and this relation between an affirmation and its denial is contradiction. An affirmation that some

63

experiences are informative of properties of realities other than experiences contradicts the affirmation that no experiences are so informative.

The disbelief, however, that there are informing experiences is not a matter of logic, but of reflecting on the nature of experience. Since such a disbelief is the premise from which one argues, and in defense of which he philosophizes, the logical character of his arguing constitutes only the logical consistency of his affirmations in defense of this premise. It does not establish the premise as sound. No philosophy can *establish* its own premise as sound.

When, however, experience *is believed* to be the only reality which is knowable, it logically follows that no reality other than experience *is believed* to be knowable. This belief is implied in the belief that experience is the only type of knowable reality. Descartes, for example, entertained this belief as a possible premise for a philosophy, although he did not take it seriously. He did, nevertheless, soundly point out that if one were to take this point of view, he might well doubt the reality of the "earth, the sky, the stars, and all the other objects which (he) was in the habit of perceiving by the senses." [23] It must be pointed out, however, that the statement itself of this tentative premise is inconsistent, since one cannot *at the same time* doubt the existence of "the earth, the sky, the stars" and also think of them as "objects which (he) was in the habit of perceiving."

Language has developed within a type of experience regarded as informative of realities other than experience, and this fact accounts for the difficulty which philosophers have in selecting language for defending the premise that nothing is knowable of realities other than experience. Even the term "impression" as used by Hume, for example, has a meaning incompatible with his own use of this term. Impressions are distinguished in common usage from experiences which are not impressions only in relation to realities presumed to be

64

other than experiences. Although using the term "impression," Hume, nevertheless, does not presume this distinction. So persistent, however, is the presumption of this distinction that even Hume—one of the most capable of all philosophers— is unable to formulate a philosophy which does not at times betray it.

The same must be said of Descartes when he declares, "because I was in existence a short time ago, it does not follow that I must now exist."[24] In saying this, Descartes accepts the existence of a self as a fact, even though he argues there is no evidence *within experiences* for believing there is more to the nature of the self than experiences. Descartes does not identify his existence with this experience, but takes his existence for granted as a condition for reflecting upon his experiences. Thus in maintaining that the self of which he is aware is other than his reflecting, he assumes such knowledge even when arguing that it is possible that there is no such knowledge!

Although he philosophizes about the possibility that nothing is knowable of realities other than experience, he does not seriously consider this possibility. He believes there are realities other than experience even when he attempts to argue as if he believes that experiences alone are knowable. Although he gives lip service to the possibility that "Physics, Astronomy, Medicine, and all other sciences that have for their end the consideration of composite objects are indeed of a doubtful character," he never doubts that there are such objects, and he never really doubts there is knowledge of their nature.[25] He speaks of objects whose existence he doubts only after he assumes a knowledge of their nature!

7. *Many beliefs in reasonable life are accepted on faith*

Accepting some beliefs as sound is an element in all serious reflecting. An individual, for instance, who refused to trust his "memory" would be incapable of a type of reflecting which is itself one criterion of reasonable living. Although the warrant for such trusting of memory is accepted in practice, the warrant for it is not demonstrable, because it cannot be demonstrated without first assuming it. Since demonstrating is a temporal process, one cannot undertake a demonstration without comprehending several steps as a unified procedure; and such comprehending is an instance of remembering. It would, therefore, be senseless citing such a process as demonstrating the veridical reporting of memory when comprehending the process as a demonstration is itself an instance of memory. Recalling events is one type of mental activity, and trusting a recall as a veridical report of past events is another type of mental activity. Accepting a recall as a report of past occurrence is still another type of mental activity, which is faith in the dependability of such a report. A reported account of an event may well be preserved, and used as a criterion for testing the trustworthiness of another memory report of the same event; but this type of testing of memory assumes that events recorded in the past are remembered as having occurred. Thus the trustworthiness of memory cannot be established without using memory, and in so far as one assumes the trustworthiness of memory, he does not demonstrate it so much as exemplify a property of reasonable life.

In reflecting about the justification for trusting memory, one accepts principles of logic as criteria for the rationality of reflecting. This again is circular—indicating that a condition for rational thinking is regarded as a criterion for such thinking. Since one cannot establish the justification for thinking consistently without thinking consistently, he employs a condition whose warrant he endeavors to establish. One, however, who thinks consistently, because he regards it as a contribution to "reasonable" life, does not undertake to demonstrate the warrant for the rule of consistency. He acts according to this rule as the criterion for his thinking; and

66

he acts in this way because he regards it as sound. Affirming a philosophy as a logical system consists in defending the soundness of its premise according to principles of logic which also are regarded as sound. Accepting both a premise of a philosophy and a procedure for arguing in its defense is affirming faith; and the warrant for this twofold faith is taken for granted in every philosophy. A philosophy, therefore, cannot question the soundness of the procedure of having faith in the soundness of some belief, since accepting some belief as sound is itself a condition for philosophizing.

Chapter IV

FAITH IN THE TRUTH OF RELIGIOUS AFFIRMATIONS

1. *Interpretations affirmed as religious faith denote a reality other than interpretations*

A belief about any reality is an interpretation; and a belief about a reality which is revered as ultimate is specifically a religious interpretation. An interpretation is uniquely religious if the reality interpreted as ultimate is also revered or worshiped as "the first." [1] The belief, for example, that "the Lord, the first," made "heaven and earth" is such an interpretation both of the nature of ultimate reality and of the nature of the world in relation to it. Hence in affirming that "The Lord did not create it a chaos, but formed it," one acknowledges that the world cannot be interpreted in its total context without taking account of a reality which is other than the world itself. [2] And in believing there is such a reality to which the world is related, one also believes that an affirmation of its existence is a true interpretation of the nature of the world.

Since an affirmation about "the Creator of the world" designates a reality to which the world is believed to refer, the sense of the term "Creator" is denotative. It denotes a reality affirmed in faith as "the first," "the Lord of creation," "the God of heaven," whose "glory is above earth and heaven." [3]

All words used for referring to ultimate reality have one denotative function in common; but what they do not have

68

in common are interpretations of its nature. The meaning, for example, of the expression, "The Lord, the first," is not the same as the expression, "The Lord, who made heaven and earth." Yet, the reality presumed to be denoted by both expressions is the same. An awareness of the fact, therefore, that differences in the meanings of terms do not imply different denoted realities is essential both for an understanding of the nature of language, and also for an understanding of the nature of religious faith. The reality whose nature religious life endeavors to interpret may be referred to by many names, and this fact is recognized by Cleanthes when he speaks of "God most glorious, called by many a name, nature's great king." The many names used in religious life for designating the reality revered as ultimate have diverse meanings, but nevertheless, denote one reality. When, therefore, one understands that many terms may be presumed to denote one reality, he does not make the mistaken inference that there is no common basis for religious faith from the fact that there is no single language with which religious faith is affirmed. What is of utmost significance in religious faith is not a language used for denoting a reality revered as ultimate. It is rather believing there is such a reality of which informed interpretations may be affirmed in language.

2. *Religious faith is affirmed as propositions*

The belief that there is one reality of supreme cosmic significance is the faith that it is "the first," and it is this "first" of all realities which is referred to as *the* Lord who made heaven and earth."[4] The affirmation that there is such a reality is thus a declarative sentence whose intended role is stating a proposition. An interpretation regarded as true is a proposition, and it is affirmed in language with the conviction that it is capable of being defended as true. What is believed capable of such defense as "true," therefore, is not

69

religious faith as a type of experience, but is rather propositions affirmed in faith.

Believing there is one ultimate reality of utmost cosmic significance should not be confused with naming it. Naming is selecting a particular term from the vocabulary of one's culture, and all names selected for this role are arbitrary. But revering a reality as "the first" in cosmic significance is not arbitrary. It is itself religious faith. Naming a reality is subsequent to believing it exists. Hence one does not infer the existence of a reality from naming it, but rather selects a name for denoting it when he believes there is a reality significant enough in the context of his interpretations to be given a name. *Naming* a reality revered as "the first" is, therefore, not essential to religious faith, but is rather an aspect of reducing faith to linguistic form. One might well believe there is a reality whose glory fills "the whole earth," and yet never reduce this belief to articulate form, and never assign a name to it.[5] But when one uses a name for denoting, he assumes there is a reality which he denotes by the name. Thus the definite article in the denoting expression, "the first," introduces a singular existence statement, the intention of which is affirming a belief about the status of one reality.

Existence of realities may not be inferred from the fact that names are used for denoting; but when a reality which exists is denoted by a name, the naming itself is cognitively significant. And it is the existence of the named reality which makes the denoting of it one factor in acquiring knowledge. Thus the significance of a reality for an interpreter is not determined by the name he uses for denoting the reality, but by an interpretation of it for which the name is a language equivalent.

One makes a judgment about existence when he believes there is an ultimate reality, and such a judgment is a *premise* of religious faith. Making such a judgment as an act of religious faith should not, therefore, be confused with the act

70

of affirming this judgment in language, since any act of *affirming* an interpretation is religiously significant only as it is subsequent to a *judgment* about existence. One makes a judgment about existence, for example, in affirming the religious faith that "the whole earth is full of His glory," and such an existence judgment is one aspect of the meaning of the expression, "God, the Creator." In making such a judgment, however, a person's attention is primarily centered on the reality he presumes to interpret rather than on his interpretation. All interpreting, therefore, is a grave matter for an individual who earnestly wants to believe only true interpretations. And it is this aspect of a religious person's life which confronts him with a problem much more grave than any language activity. It is having interpretations which are true, so that language selected for stating them will be informed. The supreme concern of religious life, for example, which affirms the faith that there is a "Creator of heaven and earth" is that there is a reality which corresponds to this descriptive phrase. This concern, however, is not primarily with language. It is rather with the truth of interpretations which may, or may not, be reduced to language. But when they are reduced to language, it is always in declarative sentences stating judgments about existence.

Since religious faith is an interpretation of life and the world in relation to ultimate reality, religious faith is cognitively significant only if more than language is known. When cognitively significant, according to this criterion, religious faith includes interpretations which are true, and acquiring such interpretations is the objective of all intellectually serious religious life. This objective, however, is not attained merely in understanding affirmations in language. It extends rather to a concern for having true interpretations. Such intended interpretations are the essence of religious faith; and their affirmation constitutes the propositions of a religious person's creed.

Such propositions constituting a creed of religious faith are respected by a religious person only because they are regarded by him as true; and their truth is not a function of the language with which they are affirmed. It is rather a property of the interpretation which is affirmed. The intention of religious life is interpreting ultimate reality, and every interpretation of it which a religious person takes seriously is regarded by him as informed of its nature. Regarding it as informed, however, is a feature of faith, whereas the actual informative character of belief is its adequacy for interpreting reality.

3. *Affirmations of religious faith are regarded as true*

One regards interpretations as true in the very act of seriously affirming them. Hence a religious person regards his interpretations of the nature of ultimate reality as true in affirming them as the creed of his faith. Such an evaluation of interpretations, of course, is only an estimate of their truth; and is not a criterion of their truth. Their truth is their cognitive character, whereas an *estimate* of their truth is what is thought about their cognitive character. Only when interpretations are thought to be true are they seriously affirmed, and so only when interpretations of ultimate reality are thought to be true are they included in the creed of religious faith.

A person may, of course, be *confident* that an interpretation is true when it is not true, and in this case, his confidence is unfounded. Hence the possible disparity between interpretations and their truth confronts every reflective person with a grave problem of ascertaining which interpretations he regards as true actually are true. No person who has thought about this problem is satisfied to believe that the most significant factor in religious life is a *conviction* that interpretations are true. It is rather the warrant for such a conviction, or the justification for regarding interpretations as true. A conviction that a belief is true is only a condition for respecting it as true, and such a condition should not be confused with a justification for regarding it as true, since the sole justification for regarding a belief as true is *its* cognitive character. Another way of saying this is that a person is not justified in believing an interpretation is true unless *it* is true; and therefore, the primary problem for a reflectively serious person is doing all he can to ascertain which interpretations he may respect as true.

An assurance that a belief is true, however, is often mistakenly regarded as a condition for knowledge; whereas it is only a condition for *classifying* a belief as knowledge. Although one would not classify a belief as knowledge unless he regarded it as true, being assured that it is true is not a condition for its truth. It is a condition only for being confident that it qualifies as knowledge. One classifies a belief as knowledge only when he assumes there is sufficient evidence for substantiating such a classification; and what he considers "sufficient substantiation" is in turn his interpretation of conditions for determining the truth of such a belief. A belief regarded as "substantiated in the light of evidence" is thought to justify a classification that it is true; yet, such a classification is not the criterion of truth. It is only an expression of what is thought about the cognitive character of interpretations. Hence, one cannot be too cautious in distinguishing an *assurance* that interpretations are true from their actual truth.

An individual who respects knowledge as a supreme good in life would not admit any interpretations into his creed of religious faith which he did not respect as true. Yet such respect is only a criterion by which he selects and rejects interpretations; and it is not a criterion by means of which he is necessarily enabled to know which interpretations are worthy of his respect. An individual's conviction that reality

73

is knowable, however, sustains his efforts in finding out which interpretations of it are true; and such efforts are one aspect of religious faith.

An individual's religion includes every aspect of his life which contributes to his reverence for a reality he esteems as ultimate. It consequently includes every mental capacity he has for reflecting about the reality he reveres as ultimate. Reflecting, however, is sometimes disparaged as foreign to religious life on the ground that it "separates" a person from the reality he interprets. When reflecting is interpreted by this pictorial term "separate," the term itself suggests a "cutting off" of a person from the reality about which he reflects, and such a suggestion distresses a religious person because it repudiates what he regards as the very nature of religious life.

The disparagement of reflecting on the ground that it "cuts a person off" from the reality about which he reflects rests upon a needlessly spatial interpretation. Reflecting is as much a *uniting* of a subject with an object to which attention is given as it is a *separating* of the two. In fact, neither analogy —uniting or separating—is satisfactory for analyzing the nature of reflecting when either analogy is spatially interpreted. Reflecting is not spatial, and any term which conveys a connotation of spatial relations is unsuited for interpreting it. A reflective distinction is only *like* a separating of one reality from another, just as it is only *like* a uniting of one reality with another.

The quality of life referred to as "religious" is not reflecting. Yet, without reflecting there could be no reverence for a reality acknowledged as worthy of man's worship, since acknowledging a reality as worthy of man's worship is an interpretation—which is an aspect of reflecting. In recognizing, however, that there is no religious life without some reflecting, one should not conclude that religion is an aspect of reflecting, since this would be identifying religious life with an understanding of creeds, or with a comprehension of doctrines.

74

Such an insistence that there is no religion apart from doctrine was stressed in Scholasticism, and in reacting to this needless overemphasis, reflecting itself was dismissed as unessential— or even as antagonistic to religious life. In this tragic reaction, however, religious life was again misinterpreted.

4. Interpretations affirmed in religious faith are synthetic propositions

What is believed about ultimate reality constitutes theological constructs, the totality of which is the history of theology. These constructs, however, are no more informative of the nature of ultimate reality than religious faith is enlightened of it. Hence theologies are informed only in so far as religious faith is informed; and they are cognitively significant only to the extent that they restate the meaning of such informed interpretations constituting the idea-content of religious faith. Their truth, therefore, is not a matter of the clarity of an analysis of affirmations of faith, but rather of the informative character of the premise of religious faith.

A statement which affirms an analysis only of an affirmation as a language structure is analytic. A statement, on the other hand, which affirms an interpretation of a reality believed to be other than language itself is synthetic. The intended role of every affirmation of religious faith is, therefore, synthetic. It is an interpretation of the nature of a reality believed to be other than ideas. No reflective religious person believes that the creed of his faith consists of analytic statements which are true only by definition. He believes rather that the interpretations of ultimate reality constituting his creed of faith are true by an empirical criterion, which is the reality itself interpreted in religious faith. And according to religious faith, this is not an *idea* of God. It is God, of whose nature a religious person endeavors to have true ideas.

A theology which clarifies the meanings of affirmation of

religious faith may, however, be both analytically true and also synthetically true. It is synthetically true in so far as it analyzes interpretations which are *enlightened* of the nature of God. It is analytically true when it clarifies what is *believed* about God's nature. Unless what is believed about His nature is, however, informed of His nature, beliefs have no empirical knowledge significance; and a theological system which expands such beliefs into a coherent verbal system would be cognitively vacuous if it were only analytic.

It may well be the case that there are some theologies which are purely analytic, just as it is the case that there are some geometries which are purely analytic. But it must be acknowleged that *if* there is a geometry which includes empirically significant postulates, then that one geometry would substantiate the belief that geometries are not exclusively analytic. It would indeed be hasty, for instance, to conclude that all the postulates in Euclid's geometry are *only* analytic because the fifth postulate in his system is purely analytic.

Postulates of a mathematical system which are not applicable to a context other than the system itself are analytic; although postulates which are applicable to a non-symbolic context are synthetic. The belief that at least one postulate in Euclid's system is descriptive of a spatial character of the physical world is thus an expression of confidence that such a postulate refers beyond the geometrical system itself. And in so far as it does, it performs a denotative function—denoting an aspect of the physical world about which it affirms a description. The measure of its empirical significance is, therefore, the adequacy of its descriptive role, which is also the empirical criterion of its cognitive value.

Maintaining that *if* a geometrical postulate were to describe a feature of the physical world it would be synthetically true, is not saying that there is any such postulate in any known geometry, since it may well be the case that no geometries so far formulated include any such synthetically significant postulates. Yet, the *possibility* that such postulates may be affirmed is sufficient basis for sustaining efforts in developing conceptual systems which at least may in part enlighten of the nature of the world.

The premise of religious faith is regarded as a true interpretation by a person who earnestly affirms it, and its explication is synthetically true *if* the premise itself is factually true. Hence, if there is at least one factually true premise analyzed in a theological system, then there is at least one empirically sound basis for a theology. The provisional character of this hypothetical statement should not, however, be looked upon as an expression of doubt that there is such a premise, and so such a theology: It is merely a *statement* of a condition for a factually true theology.

It must always be acknowledged that the premise of religious faith is capable of being doubted. It it were not, it would not be *empirically* significant, and it would not be a claim to knowledge about a reality other than a concept. Hence the truth of religious interpretations must always remain a *philosophical* problem; and this problem will persist so long as men reflect about the cognitive significance of religious faith. A person's confidence in the truth of faith does not justify his faith as cognitively significant, although endeavoring to ascertain such justification will always be a primary motive in religious life. Anyone can classify particular interpretations as true, and when he does, he regards them as knowledge; but no one aware of the nature of empirical knowledge would presume that he *knows* which of his religious interpretations are true. This would be presuming normative metaphysical knowledge; and there is no such normative knowledge within the range of human experience. This norm is an ideal—specifying what would be known if one were justified in classifying metaphysical or theological interpretations as knowledge.

Interpretations which are seriously affirmed in metaphysics

and in the sciences are assumed to be sound; and estimates of their soundness are always in relation to what is presumed knowledge. There is, therefore, always a possibility that one is insufficiently informed in estimating the warrant both of particular interpretations, and also of the body of interpretations by which he regards them as warranted. Everyone who presumes to have a warranted interpretation of reality has, of course, different amounts of knowledge, or of presumed knowledge, and so is in a sense differently equipped for interpreting reality. Auguste Comte, for example, rejected all statements about the chemical composition of stars as *empirically* meaningless on the basis of the fact that no procedure *at the time* was known for testing the soundness of such statements. Another equally influential philosopher of science, Ernst Mach, rejected the atomic theory in chemistry and physics because at the time, he believed it was *in principle* incapable of being empirically substantiated. One must acknowledge, therefore, that interpretations regarded at one time as unsound according to the criterion of what is presumed known are at a later time regarded as sound according to a criterion of what is then presumed known.

Any interpretation regarded as sound may be respected as reasonable in light of what is known, even though it may subsequently be rejected as unsound. Men can't be held accountable for not being omniscient, but only for not knowing all that is possible for them to know; and such knowing efforts are always dated. Kelvin, for example, once believed that the sun's energy was derived from meteors, although later he himself rejected this hypothesis, and accepted Helmholz's view of the conversion of the sun's mass into radiation.

Means for acquiring data in empirical sciences are technical, and consequently, the knowledge significance of interpreted data is no greater than the effectiveness of technical means for acquiring data. Only recently, for example, the spectrohelioscope enabled scientists to study the hydrogen

78

component in the sun's atmosphere as it could not have been studied previously. So likewise, it is only since the invention of rockets equipped with cameras, spectrographs, and radio transmitters that evidence has been acquired for the presence of ultra-violet frequencies reaching the earth from the sun. And only as recording devices have penetrated beyond the ozone layer of the earth's atmosphere has it technically been possible for scientists empirically to study the sun's radiation.

Empirically significant knowledge is achievable only upon certain specified conditions, and until these conditions are fulfilled, such knowledge is only a possibility. And just how much such possible knowledge is yet to be achieved is obviously something which cannot now be known. Even the range of possible knowledge is not within the scope of present knowledge. And the reason for this is that such knowledge is contingent upon techniques which are not yet even conceived. The extent of possible knowledge can only be imagined by means of analogy. When one compares, for instance, the devices now being used in research with those used a couple of decades or more ago, he has some notion of the possibilities for future research, even though he has no specific idea what such research will be. And one cannot have a more detailed idea of what such research will be than he has an awareness of the specific methods of conducting it. This, however, is technical, and hence is dependent upon the extent of inventions yet to be made. There was, for example, no *technical* means for getting an undistorted impression of the corona of the sun before Lyon invented his camera—the principle of which is reducing the scatter of light, and so preventing the formation of an "instrumental halo," produced by the instrument itself. Thus the actual invention of this camera has established a new criterion for ascertaining which photographs of the corona are informative of the sun's nature rather than of the nature of the lens with which photographs of the sun are made.

Being aware that knowledge is attained only upon certain conditions is also understanding something of the moral responsibility with which all are confronted in the knowledge quest of human life. One is responsible for being aware of those conditions which must be fulfilled in order to be informed of the nature of a reality he desires to know. This is a problem with which earnest scientists are confronted, and it is also a problem with which all devout religious life is confronted. Every condition which can be fulfilled for extending the scope of knowledge confronts men with a responsibility. It is understanding what these conditions are so that by fulfilling them, men may actually achieve knowledge.

5. *All knowledge-claims may be stated as hypotheses*

Hypotheses in physical science are interpretations regarded as possible knowledge; and hesitancy in maintaining that they are actual knowledge is only a caution characterizing a critical attitude towards them. Such an attitude, however, towards interpretations is in no way a criterion of their knowledge significance. It merely expresses an awareness that interpretations may be true, while yet not known to be true; or, that interpretations may not be true, while yet believed to be true. Although interpretations are never seriously affirmed unless they are believed to have knowledge-value, believing that interpretations have such value is only an attitude towards them, and it is not a criterion for ascertaining the justification for having such an attitude.

Affirmations are language constructions, and although some may be presumed to be true, they need not be asserted with unqualified confidence. Affirmations of this type are commonly referred to as "hypotheses"; and when hypotheses are defined as affirmations seriously regarded for their possible knowledge value, all assumed knowledge may be stated in hypothetical form. In maintaining this, one does not evaluate

80

the actual knowledge-worth of such affirmations, but merely recognizes that although they are presumed to be sound, they may, nevertheless, not justify such a presumption; and for this reason, may not with warrant be *classified* as knowledge. Hence it is the possibility of being mistaken in *classifying* interpretations as knowledge which justifies the classification of all knowledge-claims as hypotheses. In any such classification, of course, the actual unsoundness of interpretations is not assumed, but only the inability of knowing which particular interpretations are unsound.

Even laws whose soundness is never questioned in empirical sciences may still be thought of as hypotheses because they are used in affirming *empirical* knowledge-claims. In so far as any laws are empirically significant, they may well be classified as hypotheses, since it is theoretically possible that evidence for their soundness is insufficient for justifying their classification as *no longer subject to further verifying evidence.* Thus in removing any interpretation from the category of hypothesis, one removes it from the category of *empirically* significant knowledge-claims.

The greater the difficulty in securing evidence for or against the soundness of an hypothesis, the more speculative must the hypothesis be regarded. Regarding an hypothesis as speculative is, of course, not presuming to evaluate its knowledge-value, but is merely estimating the difficulty of either confirming or disconfirming it. One problem, for example, confronting astronomers today is accounting for the high temperature of the corona of the sun; and one explanation is that interstellar dust is drawn into the corona. According to this explanation, its relatively high temperature is sustained from material external to the sun itself. In other words, it is "being heated from the top downwards." All astronomers, however, are aware of many problems entailed in this explanation—one of which is the insufficient availability of such material. Hence another hypothesis which is also considered is that the relatively high temperature of the corona can be explained in terms of the sun itself; and an observable basis for this hypothesis is the fact that the hottest regions of the corona are sunspot zones. Since, however, the photosphere—which is nearer to the central mass of the sun than the corona—has a lower temperature than the corona, a problem arises in reconciling this particular hypothesis with the second law of thermodynamics, according to which, "heat cannot flow from a cool body to a hotter body."

In realizing that the sun is the primary source of heat and light for the earth, one is also aware that its temperature is "very high." Such an estimate is relatively vague, but it is made more specific by means of methods used in modern sciences. Any such specified temperature-estimate, however, may be inaccurate, although the affirmation that it is "high" may be true. Or in other words, a temperature-estimate, such as "high" relative to the temperature of the earth may be accurate, a specific temperature-estimate in terms of some conventional scheme may be only approximately accurate. Although the approximate character of some measurements must be admitted, such an admission should not be construed as disbelieving their knowledge-value. One may well admit that an estimate of one million degrees Kelvin as the temperature of the corona of the sun is only approximately correct, and yet, be justifiably confident that the temperature measurement is exceedingly high in comparison with terrestrial temperatures. In admitting that "the true figure may be twice, or even one-half, this value" one need not even doubt the adequacy of the known methods for ascertaining such temperature, although he must admit that what is *thought about* this aspect of the atmosphere of the sun may have to be revised in light of subsequent research. Whereas any estimate of the temperature of the sun may have to be revised in light of subsequent research, it is certain that an affirmation of its

82

high temperature relative to the lower temperature of the earth will never have to be revised.

Acknowledging that a measurement, such as a temperature-estimate of the sun, is only "approximate" is not, however, the same as admitting that it is arbitrary because expressed in terms of a conventional scale. A thermometer scale is arbitrary; yet what is not arbitrary is an estimate of a property of a physical body in terms of a particular scale, such as Centigrade, Fahrenheit, or Kelvin. The cognitive significance of an estimate of the temperature of one region of the sun's atmosphere in relation to the temperature of other regions is not dependent upon a particular thermometer scale. The fact that every measuring scale is arbitrary is, therefore, not the fact which is stressed here, but rather the fact that the very instruments with which measurements are made condition the knowledge-value of estimated measurements.

An estimate likewise of the mass of the sun is cognitively significant in relation to an estimate of the mass of another body, such as the earth. The cognitive significance of such an estimate, however, is not dependent upon an expression of the estimate in an arithmetical number. Numbers are arbitrary. But what is not arbitrary is the fact that the mass of the sun may be in the neighborhood of a third of a million times greater than the mass of the earth. Affirming that "the sun contains approximately 332,000 times the amount of matter in the earth" is specifying this comparative measurement in terms of one scale—the arithmetical—and this scale is obviously conventional. But an interpretation of the amount of matter constituting the mass of the sun in comparison with the mass of the earth is not conventional.

In so far as the mass of the sun is greater than the mass of the earth, an affirmation that it is greater is true, even though an affirmation of the exact comparison may not be true. One must, therefore, distinguish the truth of an interpretation from the accuracy of a measurement which specifies a very delimited type of interpretation. No one would doubt that the age of the sun is very great; and for all who believe that the earth was somehow derived from the substance of the sun, the sun is believed to be older than the earth. Affirming this comparative age of the sun is itself implied in the belief that the earth is derived from the sun. Although no scientifically literate person would doubt the truth of the affirmation that the formation of the earth as a planet of the sun is subsequent to the existence of the sun, many may well doubt any estimate of the actual age of the sun, or any estimate of the actual age of the earth. On the basis of studies of the disintegration of uranium and other comparable elements, Rayleigh and Joly estimated that the age of the earth is less than a billion years. Other estimates place the age of the earth at three and a third billions. There obviously is a very great discrepancy in the estimates of "one billion" and "three and a third billions," and yet both of these estimates agree that the age of the earth is "very great" in comparison with human history.

It is obvious that both estimates are not accurate, although both may be stated in ways which are true propositions. If the age of the earth is estimated as not less than one billion years, it may also be estimated as approximately three and one third billion years. But if its age is estimated as not greater than a billion years, it may not also be estimated as three and a third billion years, since these estimates are contradictory of each other. There is, on the other hand, no such contradiction in maintaining that what is at least one may also be three or more.

Estimates of the age of the earth may well change, but such revisions in interpretations have nothing whatever to do with a conventional number system for affirming such estimates. The same number system used for stating one billion years as the estimated age of the earth is used for stating three and one third billion years as its estimated age. Such revision in the estimated age of the earth is a consequence of using methods which enable scientists to become acquainted with evidence with which they were not previously acquainted. As relevant evidence changes, interpretations assumed to be cognitively significant also change.

Everyone is aware that estimates of the number of stars in our galaxy have progressively changed as equipment has been devised for studying the galaxy. Not much more than twenty five years ago, the estimated number of stars in our galaxy was approximately ten billion. Now the estimate is ten times this. The estimate that there are *at least* ten billion stars in our galaxy is, however, *logically* compatible with the estimate that there are one hundred billion. But the estimate that there are ten billion *and no more* is not logically compatible with the estimate that there are one hundred billion. An estimate that there are *at least* ten billion stars is, therefore, not discredited by an extension of the estimated number, but an estimate that there are *no more than* ten billion is discredited by any increase in the estimated number.

The *language* with which interpretations are affirmed must, therefore, be carefully considered lest its cognitive significance be discredited in the course of scientific research. Even specific estimates are approximate, and their approximate character may well be acknowledged when appropriate language is selected for affirming them. Such a simple rule of language-procedure would itself do much to save men from the conclusion that *nothing* can justifiably be believed as true. An affirmation, for example, that the form of our galaxy is a "circular sheet" whose "thickness" is less than its diameter may be true, although an estimate of its diameter in terms of a hundred thousand light years may not be accurate, and so may be subject to revision in the course of subsequent research. An interpretation, on the other hand, that the "thickness" of the galaxy is less than its diameter may be a sound

85

interpretation of its form even though a specification of its thickness in terms of ten thousand light years may not be sound.

Although all scientific research is confronted by limits in the accuracy of measuring, it does not follow that such potential inaccuracy cannot progressively be reduced, and so the knowledge-significance of measurements be correspondingly increased. Even an estimate of the possible extent of inaccuracy in measurements may itself be knowledge. For example, the estimated mean distance of the sun from the earth as 93,009,000 miles may be inaccurate, and yet the estimate that this measurement is correct to about 10,000 miles may be accurate. *If* this is an accurate estimate of the range of possible error in this particular measurement, *then* knowledge is possessed of a criterion by which the knowledge-value of this measurement itself is soundly evaluated. Whether such knowledge actually is possessed is, of course, problematic!

The conditional form of statement is a *language construction,* although the set of conditions as specified in its antecedent may be other than language. The conditional statement, *"If* there is a 'weak magnetic field permeating the whole galaxy,'" is for example, an affirmation about a condition which would be sufficient to account for the formation of masses of magnetized material. In affirming this statement in astronomy, it is assumed (1) that there is such a cosmic field; (2) that there is metallic dust in this field; (3) that such magnetized dust is gravitationally attracted by other condensations; (4) that this process is conditioned by the amount of matter and by its proximity to other matter—to mention only a few of many assumptions included in this explanation of the magnetic character of stellar bodies. Although the soundness of no single assumption included in this hypothesis is doubted, the hypothesis, nevertheless, is not affirmed as knowledge, but only as possible knowledge. The

86

possibility that it qualifies as knowledge is not doubted. If it were, the hypothesis would not seriously be affirmed. The very fact, therefore, that it is seriously considered as a possible explanation for one aspect of the physical world indicates what is thought about its knowledge-value. Since its knowledge-value, however, is not known, it is stated in the form of a conditional proposition, although stating it in such a form only expresses caution with which this interpretation is *classified* as knowledge. It is not an evaluation of its actual knowledge-significance, but only an acknowledgment that such significance is not known, although presumed. And this presumption is the basis on which the interpretation is itself seriously affirmed.

Even hypotheses which are acknowledged as *experimentally untestable* are, nevertheless, sometimes regarded as reasonable knowledge-claims. The belief, for example, that a magnetic field permeates the *entire* galaxy is such an hypothesis which is believed to be sound; and on the basis of this hypothesis, it is maintained that metallic dust enters into the formation of stellar bodies. This complex set of beliefs—none of which is assumed to be experimentally testable—is stated as a conditional proposition: "*If* a large mass of this dust were to condense to form a star, the star would begin its life strongly magnetized."[6] The affirmation that such a mass would be magnetized by virtue of consisting of magnetized material is, of course, analytic. Yet, the cognitive significance of this affirmation is not analytic, but synthetic, because it is assumed (1) that there is magnetized material; and (2) that it does cohere into gravitational centers.

The religious affirmation, "There is a creator of the world," likewise may be stated as a conditional proposition without in any way weakening the conviction of religious life that it is true. Using the language-form of a conditional statement is not classifying the truth of affirmed belief. It is only acknowledging that an interpretation believed to be true may be stated in ways whose testing is *conceivable;* and the belief that it could support conceivable test conditions is confidence in its truth. Although one is confident in its truth, he, nevertheless, hesitates to affirm that he *knows* it is true, since such a dogmatic pronouncement would imply that the affirmation is only analytic. The statement, *"If* there is a creator of the world, then the world is related to a reality other than itself," in no way conveys any lack of confidence in its truth. The conviction that there is such a reality is religious faith; and a trust in the *truth* of this faith is included in religious faith itself. No religious person who believes there is a reality more ultimate than the physical world believes that this affirmation of faith is only analytically true. He believes it is empirically true, because he believes it is a sound affirmation about the nature of reality. Yet, his very confidence in its cognitive significance makes him unwilling to maintain that he *knows* it is true. He believes that it is true; and believing this, he *classifies* it as knowledge.

6. *Synthetic propositions are in principle testable*

The *type* of religious interpretation considered in this study does not differ *in principle* from *some* interpretations affirmed in the empirical sciences. Yet, some interpreters of empirical methodology in the sciences maintain that interpretations of the universe affirmed in religious faith are *in principle* incompatible with the "methods and general outlook of science."[7] The soundness of this rejection of the *possibility* for the cognitive significance of such interpretations constitutes, however, a fundamental problem, and so must be considered in any philosophy of religion, such as this.

An affirmation is testable if it specifies test conditions; whereas fulfilling such conditions is a practical problem. No one would classify affirmations as testable unless he assumed a method were *conceivable* for testing them, although affirma-

88

tions may be true when methods for testing them are not known. The empirical *meaning* of an affirmation is not determined by what is done in testing its soundness, but by what *could* be done in testing it. What could be done, even though it never is done, constitutes the testability of an affirmation; and it is this feature which concerns everyone interested in the cognitive significance of empirical interpretations. An affirmation, for example, that the oceans will still be lifted towards the moon after life ends on this planet is, so far as is now known, an empirically sound statement about what will take place even though observers are absent. Observing is a method for testing the affirmation that tides occur, and a prediction about the occurrence of tides is empirically significant because tides *could* be observed *if* observers were present.

What is done in testing the soundness of propositions constitutes test procedures; whereas the fact that propositions are capable of being tested is independent of any actual testing procedures. Testing is what is done in ascertaining the soundness of affirmations; whereas the soundness of affirmations is their capacity for being confirmed by testing methods. Testable conditions, in other words, constitute the empirical meaning of synthetic propositions, while acting upon such conditions is empirically testing propositions. These are very different, and yet, the second presupposes the first, although the first does not in any way necessarily entail the second.

Ascertaining the truth of affirmations is becoming aware of evidence which substantiates them, and such awareness is a process which takes place in acting upon affirmations. An affirmation which specifies a testing process is testable; but conforming or failing to conform to such conditions is not an aspect of the meaning of the affirmation. It is an aspect only of what men do, or do not do, in ascertaining the soundness of their assumption of cognitive meaning. Thus affirmations of religious faith may be true and capable of being tested for their truth even though men do not fulfill the conditions for testing their truth.

Since more may be known in the future than is now known about testing some affirmations, the very predictions stating which affirmations can or cannot be tested are confronted by the fact of limits in knowledge. In order, therefore, that ignorance of future testing conditions should not become a criterion of empirical significance, one must define empirical meaning only as *possibility for being tested*.

Statements are empirical if test conditions are capable *in principle* of being fulfilled. The fact that conditions for testing affirmations are not conceivable at a particular time in no way constitutes an indictment of their empirical character. An affirmation is empirically significant provided it specifies nothing which cannot be found out in the future. Hence an affirmation is empirically meaningful, even though it is not likely to be verified in the foreseeable future, provided that it states no condition which is incapable of being fulfilled.

A statement, on the other hand, which is classified as "verified" is assumed to be supported by sufficient evidence. Yet, evidence which is regarded as "sufficient" for substantiating a statement is an expression of what is assumed to be known. Even the classification "scientifically accepted by authorities" is, therefore, no definitive criterion for the actual soundness of statements. It is only an indication of what is thought about their soundness. The classification of statements as "verified" should, consequently, not be confused with the criterion of actual verification. A verified statement is one actually supported by all the relevant evidence; whereas what is thought to be relevant for such verifying may be very different from what actually is relevant.

The classification "cognitively significant," therefore, presupposes a criterion of presumed knowledge. The only criterion used *in practice* for classifying affirmations according to their cognitive significance consists of other affirmations

90

which are regarded as sound in light of what is known, or believed to be known. This cautious way of interpreting cognitively significant classifications is not a cause for discouragement, but is rather a condition for preventing needless dogmatism. And when the problem of testing affirmations for their soundness is understood, there may well be less dogmatism both in the name of religion and also in the name of science.

Statements about the physical world, as well as about its relation to a reality other than itself, cannot be *known* to be true. So long as there is always the possibility for acquiring more evidence for confirming or disconfirming an interpretation, there is always the possibility that what is thought about such evidence itself may have to be revised. But it must always be acknowledged that this possibility in no way affects the truth-character of such interpretations. An interpretation believed to be true may be true, and may always continue to be confirmed by relevant evidence. In light of this possibility alone, interpretations respected as true are believed to justify this respect; and it is such confidence which underlies the affirmation of religious faith.

Although there is general agreement among philosophers that one function of language is informative, there is no comparable agreement among them on the the nature of that of which language informs. Some philosophers maintain that language informs only of language, and according to this point of view, knowledge consists in understanding conventional practice as it is stipulated in grammatical rules. Such under- of statements is the extent of knowledge according to this point of view.

Knowledge indeed is understanding, and understanding by means of language is using language for a cognitive purpose. But this characterization of knowledge as "understanding by means of language" is anything but clear, and it cannot be clarified until a philosophy of knowledge itself is specified.

This fact, however, is often ignored—for it is generally assumed that the statement, "Language is cognitive," is included in a philosophy of knowledge which is already understood.

The philosophy of knowledge, for example, that the only way for knowing a reality is understanding statements about it must be distinguished from the philosophy of knowledge that statements are the only things which are known. According to the philosophy of knowledge that "Categories of knowledge are . . . categories of language," knowledge is confined to language.[8] A very different philosophy, however, is maintained in affirming that "categories of language" are "categories of knowledge." According to the former point of view, the scope of knowledge is restricted to that aspect of experience which can be formulated in language. Or another way of saying this is that there is no knowledge unless it can be expressed by means of language.

Language, however, is only one condition for achieving knowledge, since it is a means for affirming and preserving informed interpretations. Yet, a condition for preserving true beliefs ought not to be confused with a condition for having true beliefs. It is, therefore, indefensible to maintain that "to have knowledge . . . the experiences which I have must be expressible in sentences which can be confirmed by others."[9] Confirmability is a property of affirmations, and constitutes a condition for ascertaining their truth. Interpretations, on the other hand, may be true even though they are not *affirmed*. When not affirmed, it is obvious that their truth-character cannot be tested by another. But any inability in ascertaining the soundness of affirmed beliefs ought not to be confused with a condition for their soundness.

An interpretation of any reality is a belief; and in so far as a belief about a reality is informed of its nature, the belief is true. An affirmation of it is also true. Since an affirmation is true by virtue of the informed character of affirmed belief, an affirmation is not true merely on the grounds of grammar.

92

There are many realities other than language, and interpretations of them are true if they are informed of the nature of such realities. Since an informed interpretation expressed in language is a true proposition, propositions affirmed in sentence-form are not themselves the only "objects of knowledge," or the only type of reality which is knowable. In understanding a true proposition, one knows something of an interpreted reality—an interpretation of which is the very meaning of the proposition. But this is not the same as saying: "Propositions are the raw material of knowledge."[10] That propositions are "objects of knowledge," or knowable objects, is indeed one point of view, but it is by no means the only logically defensible point of view.

What is maintained in this study is that in understanding a proposition affirmed by means of language, one knows it by virtue of a grammatical construction. The proposition affirmed by means of language, however, is not determined by the language with which it is affirmed. Language which is used for *affirming* an informed interpretation is only a means for *articulating* a proposition. Hence, the truth-character of an affirmed proposition is not a feature of its language-form, but of the interpretation which is affirmed. A true belief is an informed interpretation, and has the same cognitive significance whether or not it is affirmed by means of language. Language is not essential for having true beliefs. It is essential only for *affirming* them.

Chapter V

PARADOXICAL AFFIRMATIONS AS A
SEMANTIC PROBLEM

1. *Statements about paradox are common in discussions about religion*

Brunner declares a philosophy about language for affirming religious faith when he says: "The assertions of faith are one and all paradoxes."[1] As a philosophy about language believed to be appropriate for affirming religious faith, this generalization must, therefore, be distinguished from the fact that paradoxical language is used for affirming religious faith. Stating the fact that there are paradoxical affirmations of faith is not the same as declaring that every affirmation of faith must be in the form of a paradox. And the stipulation that it must be is implied in the generalization that if a statement affirms religious faith, it is in paradoxical form.

Anyone who has read the New Testament is familiar with the statement: "He who finds his life will lose it, and he who loses his life for my sake will find it."[2] Statements in this form are called "paradoxes," in the sense that they seem to be logically contradictory. The fact, however, that statements in this form frequently appear in the New Testament, and in other scriptures affirming religious faith, should not be confused with a dogmatic philosophy about a language for expressing religious faith. A philosophy about language is a commentary on language, and so may be referred to as a "metalanguage"; whereas the paradoxical statements about

94

which such a commentary is affirmed constitute an "object language," in the sense that they are objects about which a philosophy is affirmed.

Kierkegaard affirms: "Christianity is precisely the paradoxical."[3] Just what is referred to by this affirmation, however, is not clear. The affirmation, "Christianity is precisely the paradoxical," obviously does not mean the same as the affirmation: "Christianity . . . proclaimed itself as the paradox." The first is a classification, whereas the second is a presumed statement of fact. Even if one were, therefore, to presume an understanding of Kierkegaard's meaning of the term, "Christianity," he would, nevertheless, have no basis for presuming an understanding of Kierkegaard's meaning of the term "paradox," since Kierkegaard uses this term with more than one meaning.

Such ambiguity is common in discussions about faith in terms of paradox, as for example in Schniewind's statement: "The thought and language of the New Testament" are "often incurably paradoxical."[4] This statement is ambiguous since two very different realities are spoken about as paradoxical. One is "thought," and the other is "language." Although both thought and language are related in an integral way, they, nevertheless, should not be regarded as the same, or even as of the same order. Language is conventional, and so is arbitrary; whereas no one who esteems the thought affirmed in a scripture as true regards it as conventional or arbitrary. Yet, the thought which is essential to the Gospel, for example, is often said to be paradoxical; as well the language with which it is affirmed. Even realities interpreted in faith are said to be paradoxical; as well as statements about them. The multiple senses with which the term "paradoxical" is used thus make the term almost unintelligible, and this unintelligibility constitutes a language problem even before it constitutes a religious problem.

If there is a reality whose nature cannot be interpreted

95

by means of non-paradoxical language, then indeed non-paradoxical language would be unsuited for affirming interpretations of it. But an affirmation that such is the case presupposes a specific sense of the term "paradox." The unfortunate fact, however, is that there is no such specific sense with which this term is used in philosophies of religion. It is used in many senses. It is used in referring to language, thought, divine reality, and religion. What is said about religion and paradox, therefore, cannot be understood until the sense of the term "paradox" is clarified; and clarifying this term is a language problem. It is ascertaining the sense with which a critical word is used in discussions about religion.

Brunner, for example, says that "the most precious treasures of the Church" are "illogical truths," and maintains that it is "not out of a morbid love for the absurd and paradoxical" that they are affirmed, but that "these contradictory statements express . . . the fundamental paradox that God became man."[5] On the basis of this statement, however, it is impossible to know which is the paradox or "illogical truth" about which he speaks. Is it "contradictory statements" which are "paradoxical," or is it the Incarnation which is paradoxical? When Brunner declares, "This is the Holy of Holies of the Christian Faith," one must again ask to which paradox he refers. Does he refer to the *statement* about this occurrence of God becoming incarnate; or does he refer to the Incarnation about which paradoxical statements are made?

The Incarnation, according to Christian faith, is an occurrence; and the affirmation that there is such an occurrence is a creed of Christian faith. The truth of Christian faith in turn depends upon the fact that there is such an occurrence. Hence the truth of this faith has nothing whatever to do with the particular language-form in which it is affirmed. If, therefore, Brunner means by the "Holy of Holies of the Christian Faith" the Incarnation, or the occurrence of God manifested in Jesus,

96

the Christ, then no Christian would disagree. If, however, he means that "contradictory statements" affirming this Incarnation are "the Holy of Holies of the Christian Faith," any person who is careful with language might very soundly disagree.

Kierkegaard also uses the term "paradox" ambiguously. He apparently speaks about a language-form when he declares: "The paradox is not a transitory form of the relation of the religious in its stricter sense to the existing subject."[6] But if this is the case, one cannot help being troubled provided he believes that what is essential to Christian faith is not a particular form of language, but is the *truth* of faith. The truth of faith, however, is not a feature of language. It is a feature of an interpretation. What is of first concern, therefore, is the *truth* of faith; and the form of language in which such faith is affirmed is only a secondary concern—since one may have faith even though he does not express it in language. In maintaining the indispensability of paradox in religious faith —particularly in the Christian faith—one must, therefore, ask to which paradox reference is made. And this is a terminological matter. It is asking: "What is the sense with which this term is used?"

The fact that there is an Incarnation such as is affirmed in Christian faith is not a terminological matter, although the use of the term "paradox" for designating the Incarnation is a terminological matter. It is a matter of using a language term for referring to an occurrence which is not a language term. Since everything in Christian faith is at stake in what is *affirmed* as essential to faith, a serious interpreter of philosophies of Christian faith wants to know how the term "paradox" is used. And until he knows this, he cannot intelligently agree or disagree with Kierkegaard's affirmation: "The explanation which takes away the paradox fantastically transforms at the same time the exister into a fantastic something or other which belongs neither to time nor to eternity."[7]

One may presume in this particular instance that Kierkegaard uses the term "paradox" for designating the complex nature of man. And in acknowledging that "man's nature is . . . a tension between tendencies which attempt to negate each other," one may indeed unambiguously affirm: "Man's nature is a paradox."[8] And this aspect of man's nature has ably been characterized by F. H. Bradley when he says: "I feel in myself impulses to good in collision with impulses to bad, and I feel myself in each of them; and, whichever way I go, I satisfy myself and yet fail to do so."[9] Bradley's *analysis* of the self is stated paradoxically, and *the nature of the self* so analyzed is also said to be a paradox. The term "paradox" in these two cases is, therefore, used with very different meanings. That there is a competition of wants in the complex nature of the self is a fact. The particular way, however, this fact is affirmed is arbitrary, since one need not *affirm* that the *same* self both wants and does not want the *same* thing at the *same time* for the *same* reason. In affirming this, one *states* a contradiction, although in reformulating this interpretation, he may remove the contradiction *in the statement*. One may say that in a particular moment he wants what he cannot approve; and yet in wanting it, and also in not being able to approve it, he is torn between conflicting wants. Both wants, however, do not occur at the same time. They occur in succession, but since the temporal separation is so short, they are spoken of as taking place at the *same* time. Yet, this is careless terminology; and when one removes this inaccurate terminology *from his language,* he is able to affirm without contradiction that a person at one moment wants what at another moment that person does not want. The affirmation is contradictory that at the same time a person both wants and does not want the same thing; and such a contradiction *in affirmation* is a paradox. The contradiction *in life* about which such a paradoxical statement is affirmed is, however, a very different *type* of contradiction.

98

Since logicians use the term "paradox" for classifying a contradictory language form, it is unfortunate that interpreters of religion and morality also use the same term for referring to realities which are not language forms. Schweitzer, for instance, affirms that "the paradox which dominates our spiritual life" is the fact that "if rational thought thinks itself out to a conclusion, it arrives at something non-rational which, nevertheless, is a necessity of thought."[10] The term "paradox" as here used is ambiguous, and therefore, one is faced with a semantic problem in interpreting this affirmation. It is ascertaining what Schweitzer *means* by paradox. If he means that some realities cannot be understood in the categories of language, few indeed would disagree. But if he means that a paradoxical form of language is "a necessity of thought," many would disagree, not because they deny there are realities more complex than language categories are capable of interpreting, but because they do not believe that one particular language form is essential for affirming such interpretations.

2. *Statements about paradox are frequently ambiguous*

The paradoxical form of expression is often defended on the grounds that the complex nature of interpreted realities is "more than we can comprehend." This defense of paradox, however, is ambiguous, and so must itself be clarified. The statement, "Reality is more than we can comprehend," may be both about a *reality* other than our interpreting efforts, and also about the limits of *our capacities* for comprehending its nature. This ambiguity, therefore, must be removed before one can even understand the argument in defending paradox.

Not only is this argument defending paradox ambiguous, but the term "paradox" itself is ambiguous. Hence, no discussion about paradox can be intelligible until this ambiguity is removed. Yet, this very requirement for intelligibility is challenged by Brunner when he maintains: "A real and personal God must meet us personally . . . that is to say, by an incomprehensible revelation, if we are to know Him as a real and personal being." [11] This is indeed a paradoxical statement. It affirms both that revelation is *incomprehensible,* and also that God can be *known* in revelation. If the revelation of God were "incomprehensible," nothing of His nature could indeed be comprehended. Yet, a fundamental conviction of Christian faith is that something of God's nature is comprehensible in His revelation. What transcends men's comprehension is the full significance of such a revelation; but what men believe about it does not transcend their comprehension. What they *believe* about it is comprehensible; and it is comprehensible in the very same sense in which belief is meaningful.

Although there are no incomprehensible beliefs, there may well be realities which are incomprehensible. In so far, however, as men actually "know (God) as a real and personal being," He is revealed; and His revelation is comprehensible to the extent of *this* particular knowledge of His nature. But what is not equally comprehended of the nature of God is what is not included in such a revelation. Thus there is no incompatibility in believing that God's nature includes more than is comprehensible, and also in believing that what men know of His nature is comprehensible to them. Christian faith affirms both that there is an aspect of God's nature which is comprehensible, and also that there is more of God's nature than is known in His revelation. Although both of these convictions may be maintained without contradiction, they may, nevertheless, be stated in such a way that a contradiction is affirmed. And such is the case when it is said: "God's nature is incomprehensible, and yet is comprehended in His revelation."

The faith that God's nature is knowable by men to the extent that it is revealed to them is not, however, contradicted by the faith that God's nature is not *completely* known in His revelation to men. A Christian may believe that what is known of God's nature in Jesus, the Christ, is the nature of God which is comprehensible in Christian faith, and yet also believe that what is thus known is not the complete nature of God.

Hence in clarifying the term "incomprehensible" as it is used in statements about God's revelation, one may intelligently reject as unessential to Christian faith paradoxical *statements* about "an incomprehensible revelation." In so doing, however, he in no way doubts the soundness of Christian faith that God's nature is comprehensible within the limits of man's capacities, even though man does not comprehend all of God's nature. One must make this distinction between partial and complete knowledge even in interpreting people. No one need reasonably doubt that he knows something of the nature of his friends even though he may not sensibly presume that he understands everything of their complex nature. He may, however, justifiably be confident that what he knows of them is enough to constitute a basis for trusting them, without also believing that he knows every aspect of their complex nature. Believing there is more of God's nature than man comprehends is not the same as believing man's faith about God is incapable of being comprehended. Yet the term "incomprehensible" is used with both of these meanings; and this fact of language usage alone constitutes the basis for one's inability in understanding what Brunner means when he declares: "Faith is the incomprehensible miracle." [12]

The *fact* that there is Christian faith is not incomprehensible, since acknowledging that there is such faith is comprehending a fact in human life. In maintaining this, however, one does not also maintain that he comprehends the complex human capacity for having faith that there is a revelation of God. The use of the term "faith" for designating an essential aspect of religious life indicates that the *term* is not incom-

101

prehensible, although the reality designated by the term may be incompletely comprehended. So likewise, whatever is *believed* about God is comprehensible, although this is not maintaining that God's nature is completely comprehensible. It is only maintaining that what is *believed* about His nature is comprehensible.

One may have a belief about the existence of a reality and yet not presume completely to understand its entire nature. And in so far as one does not presume to understand it, he may classify it as "incomprehensible." Yet, in stressing the limits of his understanding, it would be better to speak of this reality as "incompletely comprehended." A deficiency in man's comprehension of a reality which is due to the limits of his capacities should not, therefore, be confused with the nature of the reality he does not know. Man's failure in comprehending the nature of God, consequently should not be converted into a theological doctrine about God's nature. And it is this specific precaution which should be taken into account in considering Kierkegaard's affirmation that God "is incomprehensible because . . . His love surpasses all understanding."[13]

The statement, "His love surpasses all understanding," admits of more than one interpretation, and so is ambiguous. It may be about the nature of God's love; or about the fact in human life that the nature of God's love surpasses *man's understanding*. One is a theological doctrine, whereas the other is an anthropological fact. These two meanings, therefore, must be distinguished; and when a statement about God's nature is distinguished from a statement about man's understanding of His nature, both may be affirmed without contradiction. It may be said, for example, that man does not completely comprehend God in the sense that the complete nature of God is "incomprehensible" to men. This sense with which "incomprehensible" is used, however, is not a theological doctrine, since it is not an assertion about God's nature.

102

It is rather an assertion about man's understanding of God's nature—which indeed is limited.

An analysis of the limitations of man's capacities should not be confused with a theological doctrine which is an interpretation of God's nature; but when they are confused, contradictory statements about the "incomprehensible" are inevitable. A language procedure for avoiding such statements is, consequently, removing the ambiguity of the term "incomprehensible."

One is faced with a similar ambiguity in Brunner's statement: "The more deeply we become aware of the reality of evil, the less can we explain it."[14] Since the fact that *we* cannot interpret it may be traced both to our inabilities and also to its nature, it is, therefore impossible to ascertain which of these two interpretations is meant by Brunner. One must, consequently, ask whether he refers to the inexplicability of evil as a property of *its* nature, or to man's inability in explaining it.

Brunner himself offers an unambiguous semantic explanation for its inexplicability when he says: "We cannot explain" evil because it is "something which will not fit into *any reasonable scheme* at all."[15] According to this analysis, our *concepts,* or rational schemata, are not adequate for interpreting its nature. So stated, this is not merely reporting a fact that we do not adequately interpret evil. It is rather offering an explanation for this fact. And the explanation is a theory about the disparity between its reality and our concepts for interpreting it.

One may indeed believe there is a type of reality which we designate by the term "evil," as well as believe that any "reasonable scheme" is not suitable for interpreting it; and yet, he need not believe that "the more we try to explain evil, the more we deny its reality." He may rather believe that the more we try to explain its nature, the more clearly

103

we become aware that our *interpretations* of it are inadequate. And he may believe that they are inadequate by virtue of the disparity between the fact of evil which we acknowledge, and what we are able to offer as an explanation for this fact.

In making a distinction between the fact that there is evil and interpretations of this fact, one may be clearly aware of the inadequacy of interpretations of the nature of evil, and yet be thoroughly aware of its reality. Yet, this acknowledged disparity between interpretations of evil and the fact of its nature may be stated paradoxically, as Brunner does, when he says: "The more anyone knows what evil is the more inexplicable does *it* become." [16] It must, however, be pointed out that if one understands that its nature cannot be comprehended within the scope of concepts, he knows something about the limits of concepts in relation to it. Thus the reality of evil may be clearly acknowledged although one does not presume clearly to "understand" it. This distinction is not contradictory, but it may be stated in a contradictory way.

In commenting upon evil and other complex realities with which serious religious life is concerned, one may be helped in recalling the wise observation of a Zen Buddhist master who declared: "Even Buddha Sakyamuni and Bodhisattva Maitreya do not understand . . . where simpleminded knaves do understand." [17] What is meant by this, of course, is that men who are aware of the limits of their understanding do not presume to understand everything, whereas those who understand little are not even aware of the limits of their understanding. This analysis is not contradictory, although it may be reduced to paradoxical form in affirming: "He who knows the most knows the least; and he who knows the least knows the most."

This paradoxical statement, however, does not arise from juxtaposing two interpretations, only one of which is sound. It arises rather from juxtaposing two true interpretations by taking liberties with language which make the interpretations

104

appear as if they were contradictory. Such apparent contradiction can, therefore, be removed by recasting the statement, and affirming: "He who knows the most among men is aware of how little he understands of all that he endeavors to interpret; whereas he who knows little in comparison is not even aware of how little he knows, and so thinks he knows much."

One may be clearly aware of the limits of his capacities for interpreting reality, and yet not use the paradoxical form of statement. And if one believes this, he obviously will not agree with Brunner that "We must either have rational clarity and simplicity or paradox." [18]

3. *The term "paradox" is ambiguous*

It is obvious that a relation between an interpreter and a reality he presumes to interpret is not the same as an interpretation of such a relation. Since, however, both are frequently classified as paradoxes, the term "paradox" is ambiguous. Yet, the ambiguity of this term is denied in a theory of language which maintains that the terms "relation" and "interpretation of relation" have the same meaning. It likewise is denied in a theory of knowledge which maintains that in understanding the identical meaning of two terms one knows the same reality. Neither theory, however, is sound, since two very different realities are designated by the term "paradox" in referring to "relation" and "interpretation of relation."

Kierkegaard uses the term "paradox" with both of these senses when he says: Faith asks "with infinite interest about a reality which is not one's own," and "this constitutes a paradoxical relationship to the paradoxical." The term "paradoxical" in this statement is thus used both for designating the nature of man's faith as a *relation* to a reality other than human life, and also for designating the *reality* to which man is related in faith.

In a semantic analysis such as this, one need not presume

105

to stipulate which usage is preferable. He needs to indicate no more than the fact that a term is used with more than one meaning, and that for this reason it is ambiguous. A term may, of course, be used with more than one meaning, as is the case with many words in common usage. But discussions in which such terms occur are never entirely intelligible. Hence a minimum semantic condition for intelligible discussions is a clarification of the senses of critical terms.

It must be acknowledged that Kierkegaard uses the term "paradox" without ambiguity when he declares: "In connection with the absolute paradox the only understanding possible is that it cannot be understood." [19] But the absence of ambiguity in this statement is not by virtue of the clarity of the term "paradox." It is rather by virtue of the adjective with which it is qualified, since one may infer from the reference to "the *absolute* paradox" that the paradox spoken about is not a relation of interpreter to an interpreted reality. It is one type of interpreted reality. After using the expression "absolute paradox" for designating the reality to which an individual is related in faith, Kierkegaard, however, declares that this reality, which is "the eternal essential truth," "*becomes* paradoxical by virtue of its relationship to an existing individual." [20] But the term "paradoxical" as used in this latter statement obviously does not designate a reality to which an individual is related in faith. It designates rather a relation which is a condition for having faith.

It was pointed out in the preceding discussion that logicians use the term "paradox" for classifying *a form of statement*. Kierkegaard also uses this term in an analogous way when he speaks about paradox as a *formal* condition for faith. This is not saying that he maintains that faith is formal. Faith, according to him, is itself religious life, and religious life occurs only when there is a certain relation between an individual and an eternal reality. One may, therefore, point out that this *type of relation* is a formal condition for faith, even though

106

faith, which constitutes religious life, is anything but formal. When Kierkegaard speaks of *becoming* paradoxical, he refers to the relation; whereas when he speaks of the reality into relation with which an individual enters in faith, he refers to "the eternal essential truth."

These two senses are not confused by a religious person; and one would hesitate to charge Kierkegaard with any such confusion. Yet, an inspection of the way Kirkegaard uses the term "paradox" makes it obvious that it has a multiplicity of meanings; and it is due to its multiple meanings that there is an inevitable confusion in interpreting his affirmations about paradox. Pointing out this fact certainly is not taking sides on any theological aspect of Kierkegaard's thought, since it is merely endeavoring to *clarify* affirmations stating his theology. A theological issue, however, is at stake when the meaning of the term "paradox" is evaluated for its adequacy in stating either the nature of faith or the nature of reality to which an individual is related in faith. Such a theological issue is entailed in Kierkegaard's affirmation, "the paradox came into being," and did so "by virtue of the relationship subsisting between the eternal truth and the existing individual." [21] What is here affirmed is that "the eternal essential truth" *came* "into juxtaposition with existence."

The affirmation, "There is an 'eternal truth,'" means there is a reality which does not undergo change. The verb form "has come," or "becomes," however, implies passage, as if the eternal reality referred to were subject to change; and it is this which is contradicted by the meaning of the term "eternal" as that which does not undergo change. An eternal reality may enter into relations with temporal realities even though it does not undergo change in doing so, and this conviction is basic to Christian faith: God did not "become" in the Incarnation in the sense of undergoing a change in His eternal nature.

The semantic procedure of urging caution in the use of

107

ambiguous words is not a part of a theology. It is only a condition which must be respected in using language for stating a theology. After respecting such a condition, one has, therefore, done nothing more than understand the nature of language. And yet, only when this is done is one prepared to use language intelligently for affirming a theology. The unfortunate consequence of ignoring this condition is that theologies and philosophies about religious faith are deficient in instructive value. Such deficiency is not necessarily due to a lack of profundity in affirmed interpretations, but rather to the handicap of using language without sufficient scrutiny—and this particular handicap is the only aspect of theologies and philosophies which is stressed in this study. Yet, small though this point may be, it is, nevertheless, of preëminent importance in removing needless confusions in discussions about the nature of religious faith.

This condition for the use of language, however, is commonly ignored. And it is most often carelessly disregarded by those who defend the paradox as *an essential form of language* for stating interpretations both of the nature of faith and also of the nature of realities whose existence is affirmed in faith. The faith, for example, that "a transcendent God (is) present and active in history" is said to be a "paradox." [22] What is a paradox, however, is the affirmation of this faith, and it is paradoxical only when the term "transcendent" means "cut off from" or "removed from." When used with this particular sense, it would be contradictory to affirm that God is both transcendent of history and also present in history. No such contradiction, on the other hand, occurs when the term "transcendent" is used with the sense of "other than," since God may be said to be *in* history even though He is *other than* history. And indeed His immanence in history is possible only in so far as He is a reality other than history itself, or other than realities having histories.

It may well be that ambiguous language must be used in

108

theologies and philosophies of religion. Yet, understanding such theologies and philosophies is needlessly handicapped when the ambiguity of language is ignored and language is used as if its meanings were entirely clear. Many language terms are not clear; and in stressing this fact, one merely points out a need for taking this fact into account in using language. The belief, however, that the nature of reality is more complex than can be interpreted in any form of language is significant both for theology and for semantics. It is significant for theology in affirming properties of reality; and it is significant for semantics in stipulating a condition for intelligible *affirmations* about reality.

The complex character of reality is often referred to as a "paradox," and, according to this usage, the term "paradox" has a meaning comparable with the term "polarity." The term "polarity," however, is never mistaken for a feature of language; whereas the term "paradox" is. It would, therefore, be helpful if the term "paradox" were used in referring to a form of language, and the term "polarity" were used for referring to a property of a complex reality—which by virtue of its complexity makes *simple* language forms unsuited for affirming adequate interpretations of its *complex* nature. Brunner, therefore, states a sound generalization when he declares: "No one doubts for a moment that the world, life, and culture are full of contradictions." And he points out a profound metaphysical problem when he asks: "How *deep* do people think this disharmony is?" [23]

The answer of metaphysical idealism to this question is: "It is possible to master this contradiction through the system of rational thought"; such as Hegel endeavored to do by means of the dialectical synthesis of opposites. Hence the resolution of contradictions, disharmonies, or polarities of which Hegel speaks is not the type of resolution with which this chapter is concerned. A metaphysic, such as Hegelian idealism, consists of affirmations about the nature of what is presumed to be

109

ultimate reality; whereas a semantic study, such as this, consists in analyzing only the language with which such interpretations are affirmed. When a semantic study is made of *affirmations* of interpretations constituting a metaphysic, it is concerned only with the grammar of metaphysics, and not with the reality presumed to be ultimate. One, therefore, should not confuse the scope of a semantic study of this type with the range of metaphysics, since a semantic study is only a prerequisite for an intelligible metaphysics.

A semantic analysis which regards paradox as a feature of language does not consist of metaphysical statements, as does a metaphysical idealism. And as a study of the conditions for meaningful language statements, a semantical analysis obviously is not prepared to evaluate the merit of such a metaphysic which maintains that all apparent contradictions are resolved in "the harmonious One and All."[24] Since the scope of semantics is language, evaluations of the cognitive merit of metaphysical interpretations of ultimate reality are outside its province. One may have a metaphysic by virtue of his interpretations of ultimate reality, and yet remain outside the range of semantic analysis provided he does not use language for stating such interpretations. Only when a language is used for stating interpretations of ultimate reality does a metaphysic come within the scope of semantics.

The Hegelian dialectic as a form of metaphysical interpretation does not, therefore, come within the scope of semantics, because the dialectical triad of thesis, antithesis, and synthesis, according to Hegel, is not a feature of language, but of thought and reality. Hegel obviously does not affirm a semantic principle when, quoted by Brunner, he maintains that "the apparently irrational element in history, the element of contradiction," can be shown to be "an illusory contradiction through the genius of dialectic." In maintaining this, he defends a metaphysic as a set of interpretations of ultimate reality, and such a metaphysic is not examined in this semantic

110

analysis. Hence the semantic procedure recommended in this study is not itself a metaphysic "rivaling" anti-rational metaphysics which defend paradox. It is a study rather of the problem of *using language* for stating interpretations—some of which may constitute anti-rational metaphysics.

The only type of contradiction which can be removed by language rules arises in the use of language; but this is not saying that the only form of contradiction occurs in the use of language. It is affirming rather that the contradictions which occur by virtue of using language come within the scope of semantics; whereas those which do not arise in this way, do not come within its scope. Hence what Kierkegaard refers to as a paradox which is other than language-form does not come within the scope of semantic analysis. The particular analysis as presented in this book, consequently, should not be construed as colliding with any theological doctrine, or, using Kierkegaard's own expression, it is not "tantamount to reducing the term paradox to a *rhetorical expression*." [25] One who understands the restricted scope of a semantic analysis does not, therefore, propose "to explain away" any contradiction which is other than a language-form.

Kierkegaard certainly is not concerned primarily with paradox as language expression, but rather with realities other than language—such as human life, religious faith, evil, the nature of God, and especially the nature of God as revealed in Jesus, the Christ. All of these concerns are either metaphysical or theological, and as such do not come within the scope of semantics as a study of language. This particular semantic study, consequently, presumes only to ascertain how the term "paradox" is used in theological discussions such as Kierkegaard's. And in so doing. it points out that the term "paradox" is itself ambiguous and that this fact accounts for the usual ambiguities in much of what is said in defending paradox as essential to religious faith and theology.

Since the very intelligibility of either a metaphysic or a

111

theology is contingent upon an intelligible use of language, the semantic caution against using paradoxical statements is not what Kierkegaard refers to as a "speculative annulment of the paradox."[26] Before one can presume to "annul" a paradox, or even intelligibly discuss the problem of paradox, he must understand the meaning of the term "paradox"; and only when he has done this is he in a position to decide whether what is designated by the term "paradox" comes within the scope either of semantics or of metaphysics.

Chapter VI

AFFIRMING RELIGIOUS FAITH WITHOUT USING PARADOXICAL LANGUAGE

1. *The paradoxical form of statement presents a syntactical problem*

A paradoxical form of expression is one type of language; and it is this type of paradox, and only this type, which comes within the scope of grammar, or syntax. When, therefore, one restricts a study of paradox to a syntactical analysis, it is obvious that he must challenge the affirmation that the *"language* of the New Testament . . . is *incurably* paradoxical."[1] There is no "incurable" or unalterable form of language. All language expressions are formed according to some rules, and can be altered in accordance with other rules.

The rule according to which paradoxical statements are formed is affirming terms with contradictory senses. The affirmation, for example, "Whoever would save his life will lose it," is paradoxical; and its paradoxical form is due to the use of terms with apparently contradictory meanings, because what is ordinarily meant by the term "save" contradicts what is ordinarily meant by the term "lose."

In affirming, however, that the life one saves is the life he loses, one is made aware of a tragic *fact* in life, since in being preoccupied with one's own life to the exclusion of its responsibility for others, one loses the ethical character of his life. Yet, before this paradoxical statement can be instructive of this stern *moral fact,* one must understand this

113

fact as it is *affirmed* in paradoxical language-form. And in so far as a paradoxical statement would enable one to understand this fact, such a statement would be effective according to a semantic criterion. It is, however, this effectiveness which is doubted in this study; and so the use of paradoxical statements for instructive purposes is challenged.

The paradoxical *form of statement* is here criticized on the basis of the semantic principle that such form is not suitable for communicating meaningful interpretations of "facts"; although if such so-called "facts" were understood, interpretations of them could be affirmed in paradoxical statements. The order is not first understanding paradoxical statements, and then by means of such understanding, understanding facts which are interpreted. The order is reverse. One understands, for example, a contradiction which exists *in life* when he understands the nature of conflict between the moral end of life and the means by which this end is often sought. But this contradiction in life is not understood by virtue of a contradictory form of statement. Only after understanding the contradiction *in life,* is one able to comprehend the moral significance of a statement affirming such a contradiction.

This chapter does not maintain that the only type of contradiction is a matter of grammar. It acknowledges that there are contradictions which are not matters of language. Yet, it maintains that contradictions in language are not effective means for understanding such non-language contradictions. When, therefore, a form of language constitutes a handicap in understanding such non-language contradictions, it must be criticized on semantic grounds. If, consequently, one is convinced that the language of Scripture is intended to perform an instructive role, he is concerned that this role should be effectively fulfilled. And it is not so fulfilled when the *language* of Scripture fails to make clear all that can be understood of its teachings for the instruction of human life.

Although Brunner is concerned with the instructive role

114

of language in Scripture, he, nevertheless, unjustifiably disparages a criticism of the paradoxical form of language in Scripture. When, therefore, he counsels that "the believing Christian" stick "to his guns" and "refuse to modify his *statement*," he defends a type of contradiction which is criticized in this chapter as a handicap to the understanding of affirmed interpretations. The criticism of paradox as presented in this chapter is confined to semantical considerations, since the only type of paradox which is discussed here is created by using language, and so can be removed by the same means. A term such as "eternal," for example, is misused in affirming: "The eternal becomes."[2] The affirmation, "The eternal becomes," is paradoxical due to predicating "becoming" of a reality whose nature *as eternal* is exclusive of becoming. Since Kierkegaard in this affirmation refers to the Incarnation, he obviously does not speak about the type of contradiction with which this chapter is concerned. Yet, in questioning whether the Incarnation actually is effectively interpreted in paradoxical language, one raises a semantic consideration, and such a consideration is urgent just because a religious consideration is seriously reflected upon.

Forming a paradoxical statement is not creating a non-language contradiction; and conversely, removing a paradoxical form of language-expression is not operating upon a non-language reality. Since syntax is only a study of rules by which language expressions are formed, a syntactical analysis of the paradoxical *form of statement* can be achieved within the scope of language itself.

The object of religious faith is not language, and it is not brought about by using language. Yet, a particular *form* of language may handicap individuals in understanding something of the nature of reality in which they have faith. And in light of this fact, the nature of language itself must be seriously considered in the educational aspect of religious institutions. The informative function of language must, con-

115

sequently, be distinguished from a non-informative function of language, and when these two functions are insufficiently differentiated, the informative role of language in scripture is frequently ignored. A statement such as "The eternal mountains were scattered, and the everlasting hills sank low," is obviously in paradoxical form.[3] Any reality which is eternal could not be altered, and anything which is everlasting would not undergo change. The *meaning,* however, affirmed in this passage is factual. It is that even mountains, which some men believe are eternal, will change. Scripture is indifferent to what men think, and such indifference is soundly justified, since many men believe much that is false, and, nevertheless, are not even aware of the falsity of their beliefs. The fact that what some men regard as eternal will be subject to dissolution is judgment upon men's ignorance. In so far, therefore, as a language affirming such judgment is dismissed as contradictory because in paradoxical form, men are needlessly handicapped in their enlightenment. And one reason for this needless handicap is grammatical. It is due to the juxtaposition of words whose meanings are incompatible.

Brunner is aware that paradoxical statements are peculiarities of language, and in commenting on *I Corinthians* 13:12, he says: "Every *statement* of faith is a riddle."[4] In making this generalization, he speaks about the same thing with which this chapter is concerned. It is a "*statement* of faith." And he himself states the doctrine of Incarnation in non-paradoxical language when he says, the Incarnation is "the coming to us of that which was from all eternity."[5] He affirms, on the other hand, the same tenet of faith in paradoxical form when he says: The Incarnation is "the entrance into history of that which, by its very nature, cannot enter into history, because it is eternal."[6] If, therefore, one believes that the first affirmation is adequate for declaring faith in the Incarnation, he will be critical of the second. And in so far as he regards the first affirmation as an adequate

116

statement of Christian faith, he will not be satisfied with the second, which in presuming to affirm the same faith, uses a form of language in which an apparent contradiction is affirmed.

A paradoxical statement, however, is sometimes confused with realities other than statements, and this confusion is common among those who defend paradox as a means for stressing the existence of realities which are not capable of being comprehended. Kierkegaard, for example, asks: "What now is the absurd?"; and answers: "The absurd is the *statement* that God has come into being" *in the sense* of "being born," since the expression, "has been born," is grammatically inappropriate in a statement about the nature of God.

The doctrine of the Incarnation, however, is not dependent upon the use of the language expression, "has been born"; and in pointing out this fact, one is not primarily discussing a doctrinal problem, but rather a problem of language. What is not of essential doctrinal significance is an *affirmation* of the Incarnation in terms borrowed from a vocabulary suitable for describing events in man's life, but not appropriate for describing the nature of the Eternal. "Being born" is an expression suitable for designating an occurrence in human life, but it is not suitable for describing an eternal reality of which man may have knowledge in the Incarnation.

The Incarnation, according to Christian faith, is a fact, yet Christian faith in the Incarnation does not depend upon a particular language such as Kierkegaard borrows from Noëtus of Smyrna, when he declares that the "absolute paradox" is the fact that "God has existed in human form, has been born, grown up, and so forth."[7] In criticizing Kierkegaard's use of language, one, therefore, is not criticizing the doctrine of the Incarnation, but is merely pointing out a most obvious fact that some language is not suitable for affirming this doctrine about an eternal reality.

The type of paradox discussed in this chapter is a problem

of syntax, and is regarded as one specific misuse of language. Language, for example, is misused in the paradoxical statement that Jesus is "a man subject to *all* the relativity of history, and yet the agent of a unique, ever present act of God."[8] This *statement* is paradoxical due to a misuse of the quantifier "all." In so far as Jesus is "the agent of a unique, ever present act of God," he is not "subject to *all* the relativity of history." If, therefore, this universal quantifier were replaced by a particular quantifier, the paradoxical form of statement would also be removed. There would then be nothing contradictory in the *affirmation* that although Jesus was "subject to the relativity of history," yet, he was also subject to what is not a relativity of history—namely, the "ever present act of God."

The very fact that commentaries upon paradoxical statements may be free from logical contradiction indicates that a paradoxical form of expression is not essential for affirming profound thought. A paradoxical expression is one particular form in which thoughts may be affirmed; but the very fact that such a form of expression requires a commentary indicates that it is not clear. In pointing out, however, that a meaning inadequately affirmed in paradoxical statements can be more clearly affirmed in non-paradoxical statements is not denying that there are real contradictions in language statements. The affirmation, for example, "Nothing exists," is a real contradiction, since the fact of the affirmation itself contradicts the meaning of the affirmation. Another paradox of this same type is the affirmation: "I cannot speak a single sentence in English." The *fact* that this sentence is affirmed obviously contradicts the *meaning* itself of the affirmation. This contradiction, however, is due to a needless constriction in the use of language. Using more words, one could say: "This single assertion is the only English sentence I can speak." The *meaning* of the above paradoxical statement is thus retained in a more expanded version. In affirming, "I

118

cannot speak a single *other* sentence in English," one states a perfectly clear meaning.

Expanding the language with which a paradoxical affirmation is made about a fact does not alter the fact. It alters only an *affirmation* about it; and this may be illustrated by Kierkegaard's affirmation about "obtaining disciples to accept and disseminate (the) doctrine of not having disciples."[9] Obtaining disciples is one fact. Teaching a "doctrine of not having any disciples" is another fact. There certainly is nothing contradictory in these two facts that there is a "doctrine of not having any disciples" and also that there are men who teach this doctrine, although what such men do contradicts what they teach.

The point of view underlying this analysis of paradoxical statements has been affirmed by the late Professor Reichenbach: "Paradoxes spring from incompleteness of language"; and "Nothing can be described adequately in an incomplete language."[10] Hence a means for removing such paradoxes is "making . . . language complete through suitable rules."

2. *Forming intelligible statements is a syntactical achievement*

Kierkegaard's *affirmation* that a philosopher is "something infinitely great, and at the same time nothing at all," is paradoxical.[11] And it is paradoxical by virtue of rules of language. The rule of language or definition which specifies the meaning of the expression "infinitely great" implies that it is contradicted by the expression "nothing at all." Thus two meaningful expressions, "great" and "nothing at all," are used in such a way that the meaning of one negates the meaning of the other; and it is this use which makes their conjunction meaningless.

A language expression must be meaningful before it may be regarded as descriptive of the nature of an interpreted reality, and the grammatical condition for such a meaningful role of language is the internal consistency of an expression.

119

Terms with exclusive meanings may not, therefore, be predicated of the *same* reality under the *same* set of conditions. There is, however, nothing internally inconsistent in affirming different descriptions of a reality, provided the reality is described under more than one set of conditions. There is nothing internally inconsistent in Bradley's statement, for example, that "we have to take reality as many, and . . . as one," and yet in doing so, we must "avoid contradiction." [12] We may refer to the totality of reality as "one," and refer to aspects of its totality as "many." The affirmation, therefore, made by Bradley is not about reality, but about a philosophical procedure. It is that a person who interprets reality must regard it both as many and also as one, and in so doing, must avoid contradiction. And such contradiction is avoidable on the condition that the aspect of reality referred to by the term "one" is distinguished from the aspect referred to by the term "many."

Although a reality interpreted in a philosophy may be other than language, it is, nevertheless, by means of language alone that interpretations of it are *stated*. And Bradley's recommendation is that in using language for this purpose we must avoid a contradiction. The contradiction spoken about is not in reality. It is in the language with which affirmations are made about reality. And since such contradiction is a form of language, it can be avoided by respecting rules of language. In so doing, one thus takes a grammar into account even before he takes the nature of reality into account. That is, before one can *state* an intelligible metaphysic, he must learn a grammar, which consists of rules for using language in ways which make language intelligible.

A criticism of the paradoxical *form of statement* as a handicap to understanding affirmed meaning is primarily semantic. A criticism of the paradoxical form of statement as unintelligible because inconsistent is, on the other hand, primarily logical. This twofold criticism is, however, in part a matter of

120

emphasis. Although a classification of paradox either as a grammatical or a logical misuse of language is arbitrary, a criticism of paradox as unintelligible is not equally arbitrary. Affirming and negating the same term is a contradiction, and being aware of such a contradiction is thinking about a use of language from the point of view of a logical criterion—a formulation of which was given by Aristotle, and regarded by him as "the most certain of all principles."[13]

Aristotle, however, affirms this principle in several ways. He maintains that it is a necessary condition (1) for the *existence* of realities independent of thought (2) for *thinking* about them; and (3) for *making affirmations* about them. He affirms the principle of contradiction as a *condition for thinking,* for example, when he declares: "It is impossible for anyone *to believe* the same thing to be and not to be." On the other hand, he affirms it as *a condition for the existence of any reality* when he declares: "It is impossible that contrary attributes should belong at the same time to the same subject."[14]

The version of Aristotle's interpretation of the principle of contradiction which is reaffirmed by modern philosophical analysis is that it is a rule for language formation. And it is this version to which Aristotle himself refers when he says "the most indisputable of all beliefs (is) that contradictory *statements* are not at the same time true."[15]

One thinks of the principle of contradiction as a presupposition for syntax when he considers it as *a condition for forming language expressions.* He thinks of it as a presupposition for semantics when he considers *the meanings of such language expressions.* And he thinks of it as a condition for thinking itself when he considers the *thought expressed in language expressions.* He thinks of this principle, furthermore, as a *condition for existence* when he considers the type of reality of whose nature one can consistently think and speak.

If, however, one were to consider only *the form of language statements,* he would be concerned with grammatical struc-

121

tures: whereas if he were concerned with such grammatical structures as means for communicating understandable interpretations, he would be concerned not only with grammatical rules, but also with the informative function of language. This is a concern that language statements are sound or true; and such concern is not primarily with grammar, or with meaning only as a function of language. It is a concern rather with the human capacity for comprehending something of the nature of interpreted reality. And in so far as an individual is interested in *affirming true interpretations* of its nature, he is concerned with as many aspects of the principle of contradiction as was Aristotle. His concern with *affirming* is an interest in language; whereas his concern with the *truth* of an affirmation is an interest in a property of interpretation which is not dependent upon language.

Since the range of the principle of contradiction is so extensive, its meaning as a philosophically significant principle is likewise inclusive. Its rich meaning, therefore, admits of considerable reduction. It can be reduced to a principle of language; to a principle of thought; and to a principle of reality other than both language and thought. The particular emphasis now current in semantics is that the principle of contradiction is a condition for intelligible *language usage*. But even when it is interpreted as a semantic rule, it is defended on the ground of a preference for consistency in the use of language—and this preference is according to a logical criterion.

In defending the principle or rule of contradiction as a condition for *affirming* intelligible interpretations of reality, one likewise defends the so-called principle or rule of excluded middle. Aristotle himself clearly indicates that this principle is implied in the principle of contradicton when he declares: "Two contrary conditions cannot both obtain in one and the same individual at the same time." [16] Modern analysts, on the other hand, maintain that a property *affirmed* as belonging to

122

a particular reality cannot also be *denied* as belonging to that same reality under the *same set of conditions.* This emphasis is thus upon the *affirming* of properties, whereas Aristotle's emphasis is upon the incompatibility of *properties,* and not merely upon the incompatibility of *predicating* properties.

Aristotle, however, does not maintain that there are only two possible properties. He maintains rather that it is impossible that the same property may both characterize a reality and not characterize it under the *same set of conditions.* Hence, he points out that one is confronted with an option. One may either affirm or deny that a reality has such a property, but he may not both affirm and deny that it has the same property under the same set of conditions.

According to the principle of contradiction, the *same* property cannot both be and not be. According to the principle of excluded middle, it is either one or the other. But this is not saying that there are no other properties. Aristotle is clearly aware that "pairs of contraries have intermediates." "The intermediate between good and bad," for example, "is that which is neither the one nor the other." [17] But in declaring this, Aristotle does not maintain that there are only two categories with which all realities should be interpreted. He maintains only that *if* a person were to attribute one predicate to a reality, then he must not *at the same time and under the same set of conditions* also attribute a mutually exclusive predicate to the same reality, since in so doing, he would contradict what he himself affirms. Such a predication would be unintelligible because it would be impossible to know whether the affirmation or its negation should seriously be considered—and it is impossible seriously to consider both as meaningful.

Contradictory statements are not meaningful. They affirm two senses—one of which negates the other. In such a situation, a person is left with a statement whose meaning is vacuous, and it is vacuous on the grounds of a logical prin-

123

ciple that the meaningful character of a statement is cancelled when it includes both an affirmation and also a negation of the *same* term. Whereas an affirmation of a term may be meaningful, its negation under the same set of conditions cancels such affirmed meaning; and it is this linguistic confusion which is intolerable for anyone who respects language for its informative function.

In clarifying this language confusion on the grounds of a logical principle of consistency, or non-contradiction, however, nothing is stipulated about the possible range of terms which may be used for interpreting reality. In respecting the principle of contradiction as a rule stipulating language usage, or as a condition for thinking about reality, or even as a condition for reality, one does not maintain that there are two and only two possible interpretations of reality. In speaking about colors, for example, Aristotle declares: "There is no reason why there should not be one or more intermediates between the contraries." [18] Everything of which a color term may be predicated need not be either a color or its contrary. It need not, for example, be either red or green. Yet, a reality of which the color term "red" may be meaningfully predicated should not also be said under *the same set of conditions* to be mutually exclusive of red. If the term "red" is an appropriate predicate, then a term whose sense is logically incompatible with the term "red" should not also be predicated under the *same* conditions. This is not prescribing the restriction of interpretations to two categories. It is merely specifying a condition under which such categories are meaningful in interpretations as well as in affirmations of interpretations. One may use hundreds of terms in interpreting the color significance of the rich world to which he is related. But he may not predicate a color to a set of conditions at *the same time* that he denies that such a set of conditions has that color. This is imposing a requirement both upon what is affirmed and upon what is thought about a reality which is interpreted.

124

And in so far as one is interested in the truth of what is thought about such a reality, he is concerned not only with with what he says about it, but also with the reality about which he speaks.

In acknowledging all this, one does not delimit the range of what can be thought or can be said to two categories. People who can think only in two categories do not do so in respect to a requirement of logic, but by virtue of the poverty of their intelligence. A person, for example, who knows of only two theories for interpreting the physical basis of light supposes that if light is not interpreted according to Newton's construct of particles, it *must* be interpreted according to Huygens' construct of waves. But if one has knowledge comparable with Maxwell, he need not think of it as either one or the other; and he need not think of it as both being what it is and also not being what it is. This is respecting the principle of contradiction as a generalization about the nature of realities interpreted in scientific *constructs*. It is also regarding the principle of contradiction as a condition for thinking about such *reality*; and it is also considering it as a rule for *using language in affirming* what one thinks about reality.

The motives for rejecting logic and for discrediting its principles are many, one of which is defending a mystical type of philosophy, such as is basic to metaphysical monisms which maintain "the identity of subject and object, the unity of thought and being." [19] Whereas a metaphysical monist rejects the principle of contradiction as a condition by which men falsely interpret reality in differentiating one thing from another, Kierkegaard rejects it on the grounds of a different metaphysic. He maintains: "Existence separates, and holds the various moments of existence discretely apart," while only systematic thought "brings them together." [20] But this is obviously a criticism of one metaphysic on the basis of another metaphysic. The argument in this chapter, on the other hand, is that the principle of contradiction is a language problem before it is a metaphysical problem; and it is this prior problem alone which is analyzed in this chapter.

Reason itself is frequently disparaged by those who reject the principle of contradiction as a condition for intelligibility either in thinking or in using language. Such a disparagement of reason, however, follows only when the principle of contradiction has been thought of as the *sole* criterion of rationality. Yet, when it is so regarded, it is not understood either as a rule for using language or as a condition for thinking. It, therefore, is understandable that almost anything is said in disparaging "reason," and this is a procedure of long standing which is periodically revived. It is revived, however, primarily by those who misinterpret the principle of contradiction, and then misinterpret the nature of reason by identifying it with such a misinterpreted principle.

It is this type of interpretation which accounts for an analysis of religious faith as irrational or as paradoxical when it is said to be "a real knowledge of a Being whose nature is yet above knowledge." What is affirmed about such knowledge, however, is denied by what is affirmed about the nature of reality presumed to be known, and so the *affirmation* is "irrational" or paradoxical. Brunner likewise affirms such an "irrational" or internally inconsistent statement when he declares: "Faith only exists where there is nothing to be seen." [21] In saying this, he does not, however, interpret religious faith; since faith is sustained on the basis of evidence, even though the evidence respected by religious life as sufficient for justifying faith is not of the order of things "seen." The word, "seen," as used by Brunner is ambiguous, and so religious faith itself cannot be clearly described by it, as is illustrated in his affirmation: "There is nothing to be *seen,* for it is *seeing* in the dark." The double talk of seeing where there is "nothing to be seen," however, is a play on words; and the verbal quibble is in the form of a paradoxical statement.

Brunner, on the other hand, acknowledges that "*statements*

126

of faith . . . are paradoxical," or irrational, when he declares: "The hall-mark of logical inconsistency clings to all genuine *pronouncements* of faith." [22] What is urged in this chapter, however, is that one should not confuse a paradoxical *form of statement,* or pronouncement, with a reality other than a language-form. Yet, Brunner seems to do this, for after maintaining that "the *assertions* of faith are one and all paradoxes," he declares: "The 'natural' man takes offence at them, for they are mysteries in which God reveals Himself as the Incomprehensible." [23]

This doctrine about the paradoxical *form of statement* is here rejected as arbitrary and unsound solely on the ground that the paradoxical use of language is not one of the mysteries essential to religious life. It is a peculiarity of man's grammar; and in maintaining this one does not speak about realities other than language. He speaks only about what some man *say* about them. What is said about them is a human matter, and for an analysis of what men *say* about them, one need understand only grammar or the rules of syntax by which language is formed.

3. *The syntactical criticism of paradox is on the basis of logical principles*

A definition of the term "temporal," for example, is one rule of language; and a definition of the term "eternal" as "time-independent" is another rule of language. Both terms, therefore, may be used in intelligible statements only when each term is used with a sense exclusive of the other. A statement, however, would be unintelligible if the *same* reality were said to be both temporal and not temporal under the *same* circumstances; and the statement would be unintelligible because it would be incompatible with the rules stipulating the sense of these two terms. Affirming "temporal," for example, of the same set of conditions of which "non-temporal," or "time-independent" is affirmed is, in fact, meaningless because the senses of both terms are ignored. The *meaninglessness of such an affirmation,* consequently, can be recognized by taking into account nothing more than two grammatical rules, whereas *the consistency of these rules in relation to each other* would not be recognized unless one were aware of a criterion other than the intelligibility of both as definitions. Each definition is intelligible, or capable of being understood independent of the other. Yet, each defined term is intelligible in relation to the other only so long as they are not affirmed of the same set of circumstances. When one understands the definition of the term "temporal," he also understands that the set of circumstances referred to as "temporal" may not also be referred to as "not temporal."

But understanding that a term which has one sense cannot also at the same time not have that sense is understanding language according to a logical criterion. And this criterion of consistency is prior to rules of grammar, since a grammar is intelligible only if its rules are consistent with each other. In pointing out this fact, one does not raise a question of the genetic priority of logic to grammar. He merely points out that a condition for the clarity of single rules of language is not of the same order as a condition for the coherence of a set of such rules. Rules of grammar are stipulated for the purpose of constructing language; whereas constructing an intelligible grammar consisting of such rules, presupposes the the logical rule of consistency.

Understanding why men require consistency in discourse is neither within the scope of grammar nor of logic. Yet if one is aware that one requirement of human life is communicating consistently by means of language, he desires to reflect upon the conditions by which this is accomplished. And in reflecting upon such conditions, he takes account of rules for using language intelligibly. In reflecting, however, upon the requirement for intelligibility in language—in distinction to using

128

language intelligibly—one becomes aware of a peculiar demand of life, and such a demand may be called "logical" or "rational" or "reasonable." But whatever term is used for classifying this demand, the term should have a meaning which is distinguishable from the meaning of a term describing a rule *for using language* intelligibly. The desire for communicating intelligibly is not logical, and it is not grammatical. It is a peculiarity of human life, and is essential to *some* human life. What is not essential to such human life, however, is a particular grammar, since there are many grammars by means of which men may intelligibly communicate.

In maintaining that the demand for intelligibility according to the criterion of consistency is a feature of a *type* of mentality, one does not affirm that it is the nature of "the human mind"! There obviously are individuals who are not disturbed by inconsistency in discourse; and the very fact that paradoxical language is affirmed and defended in theologies and philosophies is evidence that there are individuals who do not require consistency in discourse.

The fact, however, that some do require consistency in language is the reason that studies such as this analyze conditions for fulfilling this requirement. If no one required intelligibility in discourse, there would obviously be no justification for sustaining reflection on conditions for achieving it. Achieving such intelligibility would then be only an incidental matter. But the person who finds unintelligibility in discourse intolerable does not look upon inconsistency in language usage as incidental. It is intolerable for him, because from his point of view, inconsistency in language is tantamount to meaningless assertions. And a person who believes there is much of importance worth communicating is not content to forego any opportunities for benefiting from such instructive communication. When he cannot be instructed by means of inconsistent language, he, therefore, protests, not against an incidental inconvenience, but against a violation

129

of a fundamental requirement for learning, which is using language intelligibly.

Language is intelligible, however, only when it is used in meaningful expressions; and the grammatical condition for such language is conforming to rules of consistent language usage. A definition of a term is a rule of grammar, and as such, stipulates how a term may be used in an intelligible expression. The meaning of the term "bad," for example, is conventionally opposite the meaning of the term "good." Hence, these conventional meanings are disregarded by Abailard when he declares: "It is good for a man to be bad since God may use him for a good end."[24] This statement, of course, may be clarified, and there is no limit to the number of commentaries which may be proposed for explaining what this statement means! But quite apart from any such clarifications, the fact remains that such commentaries would not even be necessary if the meaning of the statement were clear. When, however, the meaning of a statement is clarified by commentaries, rules of grammar are respected in commentaries as they are not respected in the statement needing clarification. A statement which is in need of such commentary for its understanding thus illustrates the eminent advantage of grammar!

Brunner's statement, "Right law will only exist in the Kingdom of God, where there will be no longer any law at all," is also a misuse of grammar.[25] What is meant may be that the Kingdom of God is a norm for "right law"; and yet, in such a normative reality there would be no need for laws. If this is the intended meaning, a declarative form of statement for affirming it is not grammatically appropriate. A form of statement suitable for affirming such meaning is the conditional, and in a conditional form, the statement would be: "*If* there were right laws, then they would have a character of the Kingdom of God; although in such a Kingdom there would be no need for laws." There is nothing paradoxical

130

about this conditional statement because it does not affirm existence; whereas the declarative form at least gives the impression that existence is affirmed. What is meant is not that "right law *will* only exist in the Kingdom of God," but: "*If there were* such a reality, it would be a norm for right law."

Some paradoxical statements are hardly understandable without supplementary commentary, such as Kierkegaard's statement: "The ethical teaches to venture everything for nothing." [26] This particular affirmation, however, becomes understandable by virtue of what is subsequently said about its intended meaning. In this case, the commentary is that the ethical is renouncing "the flattery of the world-historical in order to become as nothing." "Becoming as nothing in the eyes of the world, or from the point of view of most people," is certainly not the same meaning as venturing "everything for nothing." These are very different things. One who aspires to achieve a moral objective in his life is indeed willing to venture everything for its achievement—which may, however, be regarded as nothing from the point of view of others. But it is not so regarded by the person who ventures everything within his control to achieve it.

A paradoxical expression, such as venturing "everything for nothing," arrests attention; but arresting attention is not the primary purpose in affirming a statement of moral or religious faith.

A concern of a person who affirms such faith by means of language is that his *affirmations* are intelligible, since intelligible affirmations are the only language means for communicating true interpretations. Hence, intelligible affirmations are the only types of *affirmation* respected by a person who desires to communicate the *truth* of his faith. And a primary purpose for affirming faith in intelligible form is that it may be understood by those who seriously desire to be enlightened of the nature of the reality in which a person has faith. The religious doctrine of the Incarnation, for example, is that

131

God is knowable in His revelation in Jesus, the Christ. This doctrine *so stated* is intelligible according to the criteria of grammar. If, however, one were to say that the sense in which Jesus is human is also the same sense in which Jesus is not human, he would affirm an unintelligible statement. And it would be unintelligible according to a criterion of grammar. The statement that the same reality is human and also not human *under the same set of conditions* is a proposition whose meaning, however, is not even clear, because a meaning is both affirmed and negated. One may not, therefore, say it is a false proposition any more than he may say it is a true proposition. Only after its grammatical structure, consequently, has been corrected can it be judged for its truth or falsity according to a criterion which is other than grammatical.

A statement which is unintelligible is grammatically "false," or incorrectly formed, and as such, it cannot be evaluated for its cognitive significance since only a statement whose meaning is understood can be evaluated according to a criterion of factual truth or falsity. A falsely formed statement, therefore, must be distinguished from a false statement. A *falsely formed statement* is meaningless, whereas a *false statement* is meaningful, and in fact a grammatical condition for evaluating a statement either as true or false is that it is meaningful. An affirmation of faith, consequently, cannot be evaluated for its truth or its falsity until it is meaningful by a grammatical criterion. Although only meaningful statements can be evaluated for their truth or falsity, their evaluations as true or false presuppose a criterion other than grammar. A doctrine, for example, esteemed by a religious person as essential to his faith is not regarded by him as true only by a criterion of grammar, but by the criterion of the nature of reality about whose existence the doctrine is an affirmed interpretation.

Yet, any intelligible affirmation of interpretations must con-

132

form to the rules of a syntax; and a *set of such affirmations* must conform to the logical requirement of internal consistency. This is not restricting faith to language rules, but only the *language affirmations* of such faith. In so far, however, as faith is affirmed, the minimum condition for the meaningful character of its *affirmations* is both grammatical and logical. Only affirmations which are grammatically correct can be seriously considered for their truth. And the only affirmations of faith which are respected by serious religious life are those which are regarded as true. The truth in which religious life is preëminently concerned, however, is not logical truth, but factual truth. It is the fact that there is a reality such as faith declares there is.

133

Chapter VII

THE NATURE OF FACTUAL MEANING
AFFIRMED AS RELIGIOUS FAITH

1. *The meaning of language expression is its signification*

The meaning of a factual statement is its signification, or that which it signifies. This is not saying that the signification of a factual sentence is a signified reality which is other than the meaning itself of a sentence. The signification of a factual sentence is its meaning, whereas a reality signified by such a sentence is that which the sentence interprets. In the terminology of Frege, a factual sentence has a "nominatum," which is the reality referred to by the meaning of a sentence. Or in the terminology used by Carnap, a factual statement has an extension and an intension. Its intension is its meaning. Its extension is the reality to which its meaning refers. The nominatum or extension, for example, of a sentence affirming a religious interpretation of ultimate reality is the ultimate reality itself designated by the term, "The Ultimate."

2. *Factual meaning is designative*

A factual sentence performs its intended designating function only when it refers to a non-language reality, or to a property constitutive of such a reality. The property of being ultimate, for example, is the property designated by the term "ultimate." An increase in the synonyms for this term is only

134

an increase in its intension. It is not an increase in its extension. There is only one extension of the term "ultimate." It is that reality which is derived from no other reality, and any term used for designating it has a meaning which is restricted to concepts of a reality believed to exemplify the property of being underived.

Terms are designative in function only in a naming relationship, and every such naming relationship is an instance of a denoting relation. Naming an entity is selecting a language term as a sign for such an entity, and in order to restrict the latitude of such denoting terms, rules are formulated which specify limits within which they actually denote. A definition is such a restricting rule which specifies the range of a term's application, or its extension, by stipulating the type of occasion in which it may appropriately be used. And such a restriction is imposed upon terms in order to make them cognitively significant in communication. The extension, for example, of the term, "The Ultimate," is *grammatically* a single member class by virtue of the definite article, and is *factually* exhausted by that one reality which is underived. The actual exhaustion of the extension of this term, however, is not determined by grammar, but by the nature of reality.

3. *Factual meaning is a proposition*

The meaning of a sentence is the proposition it expresses. Or conversely, a proposition is the meaning of a sentence. Thus a sentence is a vehicle by which a meaning may be reduced to a form comprehensible to all who understand a particular grammar. A proposition, however, may be entertained by a person as a concept or a belief without being reduced to any language form. In other words, a person may have an idea or a belief without affirming it in language.

135

For example, one may believe that the physical world is an exemplification of a creative reality other than the physical world itself. This belief—which is essential to religious faith —is not dependent upon language, although a statement of it is obviously dependent upon language.

The meaning of a statement is not necessarily what is thought about a statement. It is rather the meaning of a statement as that meaning is affirmed. Or, in other words, it is the informative function of a statement which is comprehensible on the condition that the statement itself is fully understood. This particular analysis is common in elementary logic, according to which an inference is an expression of a mental activity in distinction to an implication, which is the warrant for such an inference. That is, an implication is not a mental activity, but a *relation* between a given statement and logically possible inferences from it. Analogously, the denoting function of a factual statement is a *relation* between a language expression and the reality designated by it. And the meaning of such an expression is a factual proposition.

4. *Declarative sentences express propositions*

As the meaning of a sentence, a proposition is designated by a sentence, and so is called the "designatum of a sentence." The designatum of a proposition—in distinction to the designatum of a sentence—is the reality interpreted by the proposition. The designatum, for example, of the sentence, "The heavens declare the glory of God," is the meaning of this statement, whereas the designatum of the proposition affirmed in this sentence is the physical world in relation to its Creator. A distinction must, therefore, be made between the reality referred to by the meaning of a sentence and the meaning conveyed by the sentence. The former is the nominatum or designatum of a proposition affirmed in a sentence, and the latter is the intension or the extension of the sentence.

136

5. *Propositions have a truth-character*

The criterion of the truth of a proposition thus is the presumed function of a proposition. The proposition, for example, "The heavens declare the glory of God," is a presumed interpretation of one aspect of the world, and of one aspect of a reality other than the world. In so far as the world refers to a reality whose nature it reveals, the affirmation that such is the case is a true proposition. Its truth obviously is not measured by the *completeness* with which either the nature of God or the nature of the world is interpreted, but only by the soundness of the interpretation of the *relation* between the world and God as a reality other than the world. Affirming, as St. Augustine does, that God is neither earth nor heaven, nor both earth and heaven, is specifying conditions which would constitute the factual truth of the affirmation that there is such an ultimate reality. The affirmation, therefore, that God is neither earth nor heaven, nor both together, is the specification of conditions on the basis of which religious faith itself is enlightened. If there is a reality as religious faith affirms, the affirmation of religious faith is a true proposition. And it is true in the sense that the reality which a religious person believes exists, actually does exist. A religious person seriously affirms an article of faith because he believes it is a true proposition, and as such, believes it is knowledge of the nature of reality.

6. *Conditions determining the truth of factual propositions are not grammatical*

A sentence is true if there is a reality such as the sentence affirms there is. The stipulation of this condition for the truth of a sentence is a rule of language, whereas a condition making a particular sentence factually true is not a rule of language, but a fact of existence. Such facts do not come within the scope of an *analysis of language*. A question, for

137

example, about the nature of the physical world comes within the province of the physical sciences, and a question about the nature of an ultimate reality comes within the province of metaphysics—one type of which is theology, the basic premise of which in turn is an affirmation of faith.

A sentence is grammatically adequate when it clearly articulates meaning, and it is grammatically inadequate when it does not do so. Such grammatical adequacy and inadequacy are properties of language for conveying meaning, and therefore are pragmatical considerations. Pragmatical criteria for using language, consequently, must carefully be distinguished from the criterion of the truth of propositions affirmed in language. A language expression which is presumed to affirm an interpretation of a reality ought to have a meaning commensurate with what is thought about an interpreted reality. This, it must be stressed, is a semantic condition, and is not a specification of what ought to be thought about an interpreted reality. What ought to be thought about any reality other than language cannot be specified in a semantics. Whatever is believed about an interpreted reality is a concept. The property of an interpretation, on the other hand, which makes the interpretation true is not a concept, but is the actual correspondence of what is presumed to be the nature of reality with the actual properties of such a reality.

7. Conditions making sentences logically equivalent are grammatical

When, for example, the expression, "God the Father," means the creator of the world, it has the same intension as the expression, "The Creator," even though an attitude of an individual toward the expression, "The Creator," is not the same as it is toward the expression, "God the Father." The fact that the expression, "God the Father," appears in a frequently recited creed may account for an emotive signifi-

138

cance which is not shared by the expression, "The Creator," even though the translation of these two expressions in non-emotive language may be identical.

Emotive peculiarities of language do not come within the scope of semantics. If they did, semantics would include psychological studies of the significance of language terms for individuals, and this in turn would include the entire science of psychoanalysis, and psychiatry in so far as language is used as a clue for interpreting behavior. The fact that individuals have preferences for particular expressions due to associations extrinsic to defining rules is psychologically significant, but not grammatically significant. The fact, for example, that a person may be emotionally ill at ease about the appropriateness of referring to the ultimate reality as "The Ultimate" rather than as "God" is psychologically significant in the sense that it reveals something about the peculiarity of a person who selects language. It does not, however, indicate anything about the unsuitability or inappropriateness of the term "The Ultimate" for designating the same reality as is designated by the term "God." Two or more expressions may be used interchangeably if they refer to the same reality. As intensionally isomorphic, they are logically equivalent even though they are not equivalent in emotive significance.

Expressions affirming logically equivalent meanings may be assigned the same extension by being used to refer to the same reality. Stipulating that they refer to the same reality is specifying a rule governing the use of language, since it is specifying their common extension. Properties of realities other than language, however, are not logically equivalent. The extension of a language expression, or its logical range, is specified by a rule of language, but a *knowledge* of the realities which come within such a stipulated range is not a matter of language rule. The extension of the term, "The Creator," for example, is decided by defining rule, whereas knowing the reality so defined is not a matter of using lan-

139

guage, or of agreeing upon language usage. Although language conventions furnish the term "God," it is religious life which provides the meanings for the term. Hence the term has no more religious significance than the meanings given it by religious faith itself. The meanings which religious faith gives this term are not conventional, and are not necessarily dependent upon language. Rather, they are dependent upon an individual's relation to the total context of reality to which he is responsive.

8. *Ascertaining the factual truth of sentences involves more than logic and grammar*

The actual designating function of language is not decided by a rule of language. Only the intended function of language for designating can be decided by such a rule. A belief that a language expression designates a reality is a presumption about language, and only language need be taken into account in classifying sentences as designative in grammatical form. But more than language must be known in order to ascertain the actual designating function of language. The presumed designative function of language thus comes within the scope of semantics, whereas the soundness of this presumption does not come within the scope of semantics.

When, however, designation is regarded exclusively as a relation between an expression and its meaning, then it does come within the scope of semantics. Yet, the *warrant* for asuming that language designates a reality other than language does not come within the scope of semantics. Semantical rules specify the realities to which a language expression refers, but ascertaining whether there are such realities as are referred to by language is not a consideration only of language. It is extending a consideration outside the field of language, and so outside the scope of logic and grammar.

Rules specifying conditions for forming sentences as mean-

140

ingful units of language are rules of formation. Rules indicating the uses of language expressions for communicating are rules of designation. Rules specifying conditions which fulfil such rules of designation are rules of truth. If rules of designation state conditions exhausted by rules of formation, then they are rules of formal or analytical truth. If, on the other hand, rules of designation state conditions which are not exhausted by rules of formation, then they imply factual criteria.

Sentences, however, could not even be classified as "factual" without presuming something about the context to which they refer. When, for example, one assumes the existence of a context other than language to which some expressions refer, he classifies expressions as factual which presumably refer to such a context, and he classifies them as factual because he believes they fulfil a denotative function. Such classifying, therefore, presupposes more than a knowledge of rules of grammar. It presupposes that rules of grammar are significant for affirming statements about realities other than language. And presuming there are such realities to which reference may be made by means of language is presuming something not only about language, but also about a non-linguistic context. This non-linguistic context to which denoting statements in the physical sciences refer is the physical world. And the non-linguistic context about which religious life affirms interpretations includes a reality which is presumed to be more inclusive than the physical world.

9. *Sentences may be declarative in form although they do not actually denote*

A sentence is declarative in form by virtue of a grammatical rule. A sentence, however, does not actually denote by virtue of a grammatical rule. It denotes only by virtue of the existence of a reality to which it refers. Sentences may, therefore,

141

be denotative in grammatical form although they do not denote anything, just as sentences may be descriptive in grammatical form even though they do not describe anything. Hence in order to avoid misconstruing a sentence which is denotative or designative in form but not in cognitive function, Frege recommends the semantic rule that every expression which is denoting in form should actually denote, and every description should actually refer to a descriptum. According to this rule, every sentence which is declarative in form would actually designate—that is, it would have a designatum, or would refer to a designated reality. Stipulating that every description should refer to a descriptum, or to that which is described—or presumably described—is stating a semantic rule. According to Tarski, however, specifying which statement is descriptive in function and which is descriptive only in form is not an *essential* procedure in semantics. The view maintained in this book, on the other hand, is that a statement which is descriptive in form but does not actually describe fails to fulfil its intended function. And on the basis of such a failure, it should not be classified as descriptive. The term "descriptive" in the metalanguage of semantics is, therefore, ambiguous. It may either refer to a reality which is described, or it may mean the describing function of a sentence even though there is no reality which actually is described. When the term is used with the second sense, the cognitive role of declarative sentences is necessarily regarded as incidental.

10. *Sentences are logically true if determined exclusively by rules for using language*

A sentence is grammatically correct if it is formed according to rules of grammar. A sentence is logically correct if it is formed according to rules of valid inference. Rules of grammar and rules of inference are semantical conditions for forming intelligible sentences. Hence all that need be taken into account in forming *intelligible* sentences are rules of grammar and logic, and so the only conditions which need be considered in ascertaining the intelligibility of sentences are semantical.

A statement is logically determinate if rules of logic alone need be taken into account in ascertaining its correctness. Another way of saying this is that a statement is logically true or analytic if it is intelligible without describing anything. Formal systems such as pure mathematics and symbolic logic consist of non-descriptive, purely analytic expressions. Since strictly formal systems are not descriptive, or factually meaningful, a differentiation must be made between formal and factual sciences. A formal system consists of statements formed according to rules specifying logically valid inferences, and so is purely deductive. Such rules of valid inference in no way specify interpretations of a formal system, or specify its application to a non-language context. A factual statement, on the other hand, affirms an interpretation of a non-language context, and so refers to realities extrinsic to a language system.

11. *Affirmations constituting a creed of religious faith are regarded by religious persons as factually true*

A strictly semantic criterion of factual statements, however, can be defined without knowing anything about facts. The term "factual," for instance, may be defined as the property of a statement whose meaning is an interpretation of a reality other than a language expression. Knowing the truth-conditions for a factual type of sentence is thus within the scope of semantics, since it is understanding only the presumed function of a designative sentence. Understanding the truth-conditions of a sentence is knowing its meaning—that is, it is knowing what it asserts, and this is a matter entirely within the scope of semantics. Semantical rules state condi-

143

tions for truth—called "truth-conditions"—but are not themselves sufficient for ascertaining the factual truth of statements. They can only specify what language conditions would have to be fulfilled if statements were factually true. And this is not presuming a knowledge of facts, but only of the grammatical structure of statements affirming interpretations which are presumed to be informed of interpreted realities.

Both factually true and factually false propositions are declarative in grammatical form. When, however, false interpretations are affirmed with the presumption that they are true, only the grammatical form of affirmations is factual—not the truth of their affirmed meaning. Since propositions are true or false, propositions do not signify themselves. Sentences signify propositions, or another way of saying this is that propositions are the signification of sentences. As stated, this is a semantic criterion of sentences, but not of propositions.

Understanding sentences or statements in religious creeds about divine reality is understanding what religious individuals believe about reality. Knowing the presumed function of language in creeds and theologies is knowing something about religious faith, and it is also knowing something about realities which religious individuals interpret, provided religious interpretations are factually true. The conviction that they are true is one aspect of religious faith, and this is the aspect of religious faith of which account should be taken in a semantical study which is regarded as a preface to a philosophy of religion.

REFERENCES

Chapter I

1. *Meaning of Meaning*, p. 158, Harcourt, 1948
2. *Magic, Science and Religion*, p. 47, Doubleday, 1954
3. *Ibid.*, p. 51
4. *Timaeus* 75E
5. *Leviathan*, Ch. XXXI
6. *Way to Wisdom*, p. 68; trans., R. Manheim; Gollancz, London, 1951
7. *Ibid.*, p. 162
8. *Ibid.*, p. 71
9. *Ibid.*, p. 69
10. *Ibid.*, p. 50
11. *Ibid.*, p. 95
12. *Ibid.*, p. 50
13. *The Mystery of Being*, vol. II, p. 83; Regnery, 1951
14. *The Philosophy of Existence*, p. 19, Philosophical Library, 1949
15. *Ibid.*, p. 23
16. *Ibid.*, p. 10
17. *The Mystery of Being*, vol. 1, p. 47
18. *Ibid.*, p. 9
19. *Summa Theologica*, Q. 1, Art. 6
20. Urban, W. M., *Language and Reality*, p. 582, Allen and Unwin, 1939
21. *Man's Right to Knowledge*, "Religion," p. 81; Columbia, 1954. Italics mine.
22. *Op. cit.*, p. 118; 126
23. *Concluding Unscientific Postscript*, p. 75, Princeton, 1944
24. Malinowski, *op. cit.*, p. 55
25. *Ibid.*, p. 67
26. *Ibid.*, p. 51
27. Peale, N. V., *The Power of Positive Thinking*, p. 31, Prentice-Hall, 1954
28. *Ibid.*, p. 121; 15

Chapter II

1. *Op. cit.,* p. 158
2. *Human Knowledge,* p. 452, Simon and Schuster, 1949
3. *Essay Concerning Human Understanding,* II, I, 2; Open Court, 1933
4. *Symbolism,* p. 16, Macmillan, 1927
5. *Prolegomena to Future Metaphysics,* p. 109, Open Court, 1933
6. *Ibid.,* p. 45. Italics mine.
7. *Ibid.,* p. 35
8. *Ibid.,* p. 103
9. *Op. cit.,* II, I, 10
10. *Op. cit.,* p. 25
11. *Ibid.,* p. 23
12. *Appearance and Reality,* p. 125, Allen and Unwin, 1925
13. *The Nature of Religion,* p. 50, Crowell, 1933
14. *Metaphysics* 981b, 10
15. *Op. cit.,* p. 43
16. *Ibid.,* p. 79
17. *Op. cit.,* IV, XI, 1
18. *Op. cit.,* p. 35
19. *Meditations on First Philosophy,* II, 41; Open Court, 1937
20. *Op. cit.,* p. 36
21. *Space, Time and Deity,* vol. II, p. 184, Macmillan, 1920
22. *Op. cit.,* p. 48
23. *Ibid.,* p. 102
24. *Op. cit.,* p. 79
25. *Ibid.,* p. 78
26. *The Philosophy of Existence,* p. 80, Philosophical Library, 1949
27. *Op. cit.,* p. 179
28. *Ibid.,* p. 179
29. *Isaiah* 44:24

Chapter III

1. *Implication and Linear Inference,* p. 61, Macmillan, London, 1920
2. *Op. cit.,* p. 45
3. *Op. cit.,* p. 4
4. *Theaetetus* 170B

5. *Philosophy of Religion,* p. 102; Trans., A. F. D. Farrer and B. L. Woolf; Ivor Nicholson and Watson, London, 1937
6. Bakewell, C. M., *Sourcebook in Ancient Philosophy,* p. 67, Holt, 1907
7. *Readings in Philosophical Analysis,* p. 162; ed. H. Feigl and W. Sellars; Appleton-Century-Crofts, 1949
8. *Op. cit.,* IV, II, 1
9. *Ibid.,* IV, I, 8
10. *Ibid.,* IV, II, 15
11. *Ibid.,* IV, II, 15
12. *Op. cit.,* p. 403
13. Ellison, M. A., *The Sun and Its Influence,* Routledge and Kegan Paul, 1955
14. *Ibid.,* p. 22
15. *System of Logic* V, IV, 5
16. *Prolegomena to any Future Metaphysics,* p. 49, Open Court, Chicago, 1933
17. *Op. cit.,* II, XXIII, 2
18. *Ibid.,* II, VIII, 24
19. *Ibid.,* II, XXIII, 10
20. *Ibid.,* II, VIII, 24
21. "The Philosophical Significance of the Theory of Relativity," *Readings in the Philosophy of Science,* p. 209; ed. H. Feigl and M. Brodbeck; Appleton-Century-Crofts, 1953
22. *Op. cit.,* VI
23. *Ibid.,* III
24. *Ibid.,* III
25. *Ibid.,* I

Chapter IV

1. *Isaiah* 41:4
2. *Ibid.,* 45:18
3. *Psalms* 148:13
4. *Ibid.,* 121:2
5. *Isaiah* 6:2
6. Ellison, E. A., *op. cit.,* p. 55
7. Feigl, H., "The Scientific Outlook: Naturalism and Humanism," *Readings in the Philosophy of Science,* p. 16

8. Urban, W. M., *Language and Reality,* p. 359, Allen and Unwin, 1939

9. *Ibid.,* p. 224

10. Feigl, H. "The Logical Character of the Prinicple of Induction," *Readings in Philosophical Analysis,* p. 302

Chapter V

1. *Op. cit.,* p. 96

2. *Matthew* 10:39

3. *Op cit.,* p. 95

4. *Kerygma and Myth,* p. 96; ed. H. W. Bartsch; trans. R. H. Fuller; S. P. C. K., London, 1954

5. *The Mediator,* p. 278

6. *Op. cit.,* p. 162

7. *Ibid.,* p. 162

8. Thompson, S., *A Modern Philosophy of Religion,* p. 188, Regnery, Chicago, 1955

9. *Ethical Studies,* p. 277, Oxford, 1927

10. *Civilization and Ethics,* p. xix, Adam and Charles Black, London, 1946

11. *Philosophy of Religion,* p. 72

12. *Ibid.,* p. 79

13. *Either Or,* vol. II, p. 14; trans., W. Lowrie; Princeton, 1946

14. *The Mediator,* p. 144

15. *Ibid.,* p. 144

16. *Ibid.,* p. 144

17. Suzuki, D. T., *An Introduction to Zen Buddhism,* p. 76, Philosophical Library, 1949

18. *The Mediator,* p. 278

19. *Concluding Unscientific Postscript,* p. 195

20. *Ibid.,* p. 183

21. *Ibid.,* p. 187

22. Schniewind, J., *op. cit.,* p. 86

23. *The Mediator,* p. 120

24. *Ibid.,* p. 120

25. *Concluding Unscientific Postscript,* p. 191

26. *Ibid.,* p. 197

Chapter VI

1. *The Mediator*, p. 107
2. *Concluding Unscientific Postscript*, p. 76
3. *Habakkuk* 3:6
4. *The Mediator*, p. 147
5. *Op. cit.*, p. 238
6. *Ibid.*, p. 238
7. *Op. cit.*, p. 194
8. Schniewind, J., *op. cit.*, p. 84
9. *Op. cit.*, p. 70
10. "The Verifiability Theory of Meaning," *Readings in the Philosophy of Science*, p. 100
11. *Op. cit.*, p. 113
12. Bradley, F. H., *Appearance and Reality*, p. 35, George Allen and Unwin, London, 1925
13. *Metaphysics* 1005b, 22
14. *Ibid.*, 1006a, 4
15. *Ibid.*, 1011b, 13
16. *Categories* 14a, 12
17. *Ibid.*, 12a, 18
18. *On the Heavens* 312, 1
19. *Op. cit.*, p. 112
20. *Ibid.*, p. 107
21. *The Mediator*, p. 338
22. *Philosophy of Religion*, p. 55
23. *Ibid.*, p. 96
24. *Ethics*, p. 42; trans. J. R. McCallum; Blackwell, Oxford, 1935
25. *The Divine Imperative*, p. 271; trans., O. Wyon; Westminister, Philadelphia, 1947
26. *Op. cit.*, p. 133

INDEX

affirmation, 13ff., 68ff., 94ff., 113ff.
  intelligible, 131
  religious faith, 13, 68, 87
  paradoxical, 94, 119
  soundness of, 89
Alexander, S., 37
ambiguity, 24, 95, 99
analogy, 79
analysis, philosophical, 4, 5, 35, 60
Aquinas, St. Thomas, 18
Aristotle, 32, 121ff.
assumption, 54, 55, 58
assurance, 73
Augustine, St., 49, 137

being, ultimate, 16
belief, truth of, 72, 93
Berkeley, G., 31, 56
Bosanquet, B., 42
Bradley, F. H., 30, 98, 120
Brunner, E., 45, 94, 96, 100ff., 116
  127

Carnap, R., 134
categories, 125
  of knowledge, 92
  of language, 92
Christianity, 95
clarification, of language, 6
classification, scientific, 90
Cleanthes, 69
cognitive-character, 73
communicating, 43, 129
Comte, A., 78
conditions, testable, 89
confirmability, 92

consistency, 53, 66, 119, 128
construct, 75, 125
content, sensed, 31ff.
context, non-linguistic, 141
contradiction, 98, 100, 105ff., 114
  118, 120, 124ff.
contraries, 123ff.
creed, 71, 74, 144
criterion, 44
  grammatical, 132
  logical, 122, 128
  of truth, 137f.
criticism, syntactical, 127

data, sensory, 31ff.
defense, dialectical, 58
definition, 75, 127, 135
demonstration, 66
Descartes, R., 62, 64ff.
designation, 134
designatum, 136
dialectic, Hegelian, 110
dogmatism, 91
dualism, 57

empiricism, 46, 47
  radical, 27
  subjectivistic, 48, 50, 53
Einstein, A., 60
estimate, 84ff.
eternal, 18
Euclid, 76
evaluation, 12
evidence, sufficient, 90
experience, 25
  immediate, 29

150

objects of, 26ff.
primitive, 47
sensory 31, 62
explanation, 81, 103
expression, paradoxical, 113, 131
extension, 134ff.

faith, 66, 68, 100ff.
  affirmations, of 9, 10, 75, 89, 94,
    113, 127, 138
  Christian, 97, 107
  formal conditions for, 106
  metaphysic of, 19
  religious, 4, 16, 21, 74, 88, 144
  scope of, 3, 9
  statement of, 117
  truth of, 97
form, grammatical, 140ff.
Frege, G., 134, 142
function designative, 35, 40, 68

God, 13, 22, 30, 75, 100ff., 130,
  132, 137
Gorgias, 45
grammar, 120, 127, 129, 140ff.
  criterion of, 132
  grounds of, 92
  rules of, 128, 140

Hegel, G. W. F., 109, 110
Hobbes, T., 13
Hume, D., 26, 27, 29, 63, 65
hypothesis, 51, 80ff.

idea, 50, 51
idealism, Hegelian, 109
immediacy, presentational, 29
implication, 136
impression, 65
inference, validity of, 142
intelligibility, 128ff.
intension, 134ff.
interpretation, 50, 53, 68, 85, 92,
  103, 124
  metaphysical, 77
  philosophical, 13

religious, 134
theological, 77
truth of, 71, 92

Kant, I., 15, 19, 26ff., 32ff., 57, 62
Kierkegaard, S., 20 , 95, 97, 102,
  105ff., 112, 115, 117, 119, 125
knowledge, 24, 34, 45, 49, 70, 77,
  80, 81, 90
  analytical, 5
  empirical, 5, 79
  material of, 93
  object of, 28
  physical, 80
  possible, 16, 86
  theory of, 4, 33, 36, 61, 92
knowledge-claim, 80, 81, 89
knowledge-value, 80, 83

language, 43, 64, 69, 72, 92, 93, 95
  cognitive function of, 15, 20
  critical study of, 23
  constructions, 80
  expressive function of, 20, 139
  form of, 108, 114, 121
  paradoxical, 96, 113, 115
  philosophy of, 7

Locke, J., 26, 27, 31, 34, 49ff., 57,
  62
logic, 3, 66, 143
  scope of, 140
  symbolic, 143

Mach, E., 78
Malinowski, B., 7ff.
Marcel, G., 16, 17, 40
meaning, 5, 89, 140
  empirical, 90
  factual, 134
  statement of, 136
measurement, 82
metalanguage, 94
metaphysic, 16, 48, 77, 109, 110
method, philosophical, 3
  scientific, 11, 12, 60

151

methodology, 45, 47
Mill, J. S., 52

naming, 35, 70
Newton, I., 125
nominatum, 134, 136

Ogden, C. K., 7, 24, 26

paradox, 94ff., 104ff., 113, 126
perception, 32, 34, 35, 52
phenomena, 35
phenomenality, 38
philosophy, 10
    analytic, 4
    egocentric, 48, 49
    normative, 44
Plato, 10
possibility, 87
postulate, 76
prayer, 22
predicament, egocentric, 46
predication, 90
premise, philosophical, 62, 66ff.
presumption, cognitive, 17, 25, 59,
    61, 81
presupposition, basic, 25
problem, language, 113, 125
    metaphysical, 126
procedure, analytical, 45
    empirical, 8
    philosophical, 120
    semantical, 25, 107
proposition, 69, 72, 93, 135, 137
    factual, 137, 144
    soundness of, 89
    synthetic, 75, 88, 89
    truth of, 9, 84
Protagoras, 44

realism, critical, 57
    direct, 30
    dualistic, 56
    versions of, 55, 61
reality, ultimate, 5, 11
reference, factual, 6

reflection, philosophical, 11
Reichenbach, H., 60, 119
relation, paradoxical, 105ff.
religion, aspect of human life, 21
    philosophy of, 4, 24, 41, 109,
        144
    psychology of, 17
    semantical study of, 6
revelation, 100ff.
reverence, 9
Russell, B., 25, 35, 37, 43

Schlick, M., 47, 50
science, philosophy of, 6
semantics, 4, 140
    scope of, 143
    study of, 144
sensa, 31
sense, object of, 27
sensation, 31, 33
    interpretation of, 32
sentence, 135, 140
    declarative, 136
    factual, 134
significance, cognitive, 63, 76, 83,
        85, 89, 90
signification, 134
Socrates, 44
solipsism, 46
    methodological, 47
statement, conditional, 86, 121, 131
    contradictiory, 96, 123, 124
    empirical, 90
    factual, 12, 143
    intelligible, 127
    paradoxical, 104, 113, 117, 126,
        131
subject, 42
subjectivism, 42ff.
    epistemological, 45
    methodological, 45
subjectivity, 42
symbol, religious, 18
syntax, 3, 118, 133
system, formal, 76, 143

152

Tarski, A., 142
terms, critical, 24, 28
testable, 88
theology, 77, 112
theory, atomic, 78
Tillich, P., 19
truth, 4, 68, 133
    analytical, 88
    character, 72, 91, 93, 137
    conditions, 143, 144
    factual, 137, 140
transcendence, 20

ultimate, 19, 71, 134ff.
unconditional, 19
understanding, 69

Vaihinger, H., 15
verification, 81
vocabulary, philosophical, 24

warrant, certification of, 9
Whitehead, A. N., 29, 43
Wobbermin, G., 30

An analysis of some of the basic problems in using language for affirming religious faith and for interpreting affirmations of religious faith. As such, it is a semantical preface to an understanding of one aspect of religion—the language aspect. A semantical analysis, therefore, is not a theology or an evaluation of the validity of theology.